C000233207

KATHERINE Z

Katherine Zachest has extensive experience in drama education, having taught at all levels from preschool to further education. She has written and directed countless children's theatre productions and has developed and facilitated drama curriculum and workshops. She has directed for children's theatre companies and co-founded The Drama Company. She has presented at international conferences, and run workshops in Cambodia and Hong Kong. She currently works in Early Childhood and for Deakin University in Melbourne, Australia.

drama games

A series of books for teachers, workshop leaders, directors and actors in need of new and dynamic activities when working in education, workshop or rehearsal.

Also available in this series
DRAMA GAMES FOR...

Chris Johnston
THOSE WHO LIKE TO SAY NO

Jessica Swale
CLASSROOMS AND WORKSHOPS
DEVISING
REHEARSALS

Thomasina Unsworth
ACTORS

*The publisher welcomes suggestions
for further titles in the series.*

Katherine Zachest

drama games

FOR YOUNG CHILDREN

Foreword by Sally Cookson

NICK HERN BOOKS
London
www.nickhernbooks.co.uk

A Nick Hern Book

DRAMA GAMES FOR YOUNG CHILDREN

First published in Great Britain in 2016
by Nick Hern Books Limited, The Glasshouse,
49a Goldhawk Road, London W12 8QP,
by arrangement with Currency Press,
PO Box 2287, Strawberry Hills, NSW 2012,
Australia, www.currency.com.au

Originally published in Australia in 2015
under the title *Drama for Early Childhood*

Cover image: iStockPhoto.com/JohannesNorpoth
Designed and typeset by
Nick Hern Books, London
Printed and bound in Great Britain by
Ashford Colour Press, Gosport, Hampshire

A CIP catalogue record for this book
is available from the British Library

ISBN   978 1 84842 561 3

For Jane,
with thanks for her support,
wisdom and guidance

FOREWORD

Children learn through playing games. Whether it's a structured game or one they've made up, it is how they discover how the world works. They play without inhibition – to them it is a serious business. It is to me too.

As a theatre-maker who devises work with companies, 'playing' is the most important element of the process. I always start each morning's rehearsal with a physical warm-up and a game of some description. By immediately getting up on our feet in the rehearsal room, our bodies, minds and imaginations are kick-started into action. We have to be present in the moment and commit to the game with the same passion a child shows when they are released into the playground at break-time. That doesn't mean we all pretend to be children – quite the opposite – but like children we take playing seriously in order to trigger the creativity in the room. On the dreaded first day of rehearsals, when there are lots of people who don't know each other, the tension and anxiety is palpable. A couple of hours of 'mucking about' – as one friend affectionately describes it – sees the atmosphere change, shoulders drop and ideas start to flow.

For ten years I worked exclusively for Travelling Light Theatre Company, making work for very young children and their families. It coincided with the time when my own children were small – and I became passionate about making early years' work. A period of research and development would precede each production and the company were lucky enough to have associations with several infant schools with whom we could collaborate and develop work. St Matthias and Dr Bell's Primary School in Fishponds, Bristol, was one such school –

and it was there that I started to appreciate the significance of play in a child's life.

For young children, play is not something that only occurs at break – it is the means by which they constantly engage, learn and investigate. Some of our most inspiring sessions came out of allowing the children to engage their imaginations without the guidance of the adults in the room. Having spent time playing games, reading stories, and singing songs, we would fill the hall with 'stuff' and observe the children play. It was mind-blowing what they created together – building dens out of rubbish, making costumes out of paper, playing instruments of cardboard, and flying with wings of bubble wrap.

I firmly believe that tapping into children's ability to play is the way to educate and inspire them to learn. Katherine Zachest understands this and her book is a fantastic tool with which to do it. It's also given me new games to take into the rehearsal room and use to release the creativity of the actors with whom I work. I'm looking forward to playing them.

Sally Cookson

Sally Cookson trained at LAMDA. She co-devised and directed Jane Eyre *and* Peter Pan *for the National Theatre, London – both co-produced with Bristol Old Vic, where she is an Associate Artist, and where her other work includes* Sleeping Beauty, Treasure Island, The Boy Who Cried Wolf, Pains of Youth *and* The Visit. *She is based in Bristol where she has also worked for Travelling Light Theatre Company for over ten years, and the Tobacco Factory. She has twice been nominated for Olivier Awards – for her productions of* Hetty Feather *by Jacqueline Wilson, and* Cinderella: A Fairy Tale, *which both transferred to the West End.*

CONTENTS

INTRODUCTION

This book came about as a result of my search for drama curriculum suitable for young children. The more I looked for good-quality and practical material, the more I discovered how little there was available. Throughout my teaching career, I have continually sought out simple, easy-to-follow lesson plans that I could read, understand and implement with little prior preparation.

There are forty lessons in this book to coincide with the approximately forty weeks of the school year. The opening lesson, *Let's Get Started*, is intended to be taught first as it will establish what is possible with your class and is a great introduction to many dramatic elements.

The lesson plans set out in this book are the culmination of many years of working with and developing curriculum in my drama classes. These lessons are designed for early childhood teachers and facilitators in any educational setting and for almost any class size. This book is designed to use, build on and then adapt to suit individual teaching styles and the children you teach. The content has been evaluated and modified and these forty lessons have been a huge success with the children and warmly received by teachers and parents.

I want to help demystify drama in the classroom, making it an achievable and enjoyable experience for both students and teachers. It is important to remember that teaching drama is not just about teaching performance skills (for example: facing out to the audience, loud and clear voices, expression and reaction). Rather, it should be a time to build on children's sense of dramatic play.

This book is written for both beginning teachers looking to incorporate some drama into their curriculum and for experienced drama educators in need of some extra material for lessons. Although the lessons are numbered, it's not necessary to work through the book sequentially. Rather, I'd recommend that you find a lesson which fits in with your current curriculum, as well as your class's interests and abilities.

I strongly encourage you to take time to reflect and record your experience, add notes, pictures, ideas and responses from the children. Continue to gather resources (for example: songs, poems, stories, websites, blogs) and other drama lesson plans to help you create a rich and invaluable teaching asset. There is a template at the end of the book, also available as a downloadable resource, and guidelines for you to create your own lesson plans (see page 323).

Teaching drama has always been one of my greatest passions, and I hope that this book allows it to become one of yours too.

Why Drama?

Learning drama at an early age will build self-esteem and develop essential life skills. Drama promotes tolerance and mutual respect as children work together to create theatre and explore imaginative experiences. Children learn and develop communication skills, creativity, self-expression and problem-solving skills. Children learn to listen, negotiate, share ideas and work collaboratively. Introducing drama at an early age is a perfect medium for exploring these skills in a safe, non-threatening environment. Drama can be particularly helpful for children who find it difficult to express themselves, or for children with learning difficulties, by providing a platform for them to develop their communication skills.

Dramatic Play

Dramatic play happens when children play pretend, and can be useful in a range of contexts. A drama lesson is a more formal experience which uses dramatic play, but is more purposeful in its intention to consolidate, explore and extend children's learning. The lessons in this book will help you to extend the natural tendency of children's 'pretend play' into a more formal drama experience. It is important that each time you teach a drama lesson you explain to your class that they are going to be 'doing drama'.

This is not to say that these lessons should replace your existing dramatic play areas. Dramatic play is where children discover and learn how to play 'make-believe' with their peers.

It is incredibly beneficial to provide opportunities for dramatic play that is entirely free from adult intervention or correction. It allows children to experiment with role-play (pretending to be someone else), build their vocabulary, and develop important social skills (for example: listening, negotiating, initiating new ideas, problem-solving in a team). The teacher, by observing the play as it unfolds, can better understand the children, their strengths (or difficulties) and their interests.

It is often debated about how, if and when the teacher should intervene with play. If the teacher offers a new prop or idea to enhance the play, the life of the improvised drama can be greatly extended or attract other children to join in. A teacher can also offer a more challenging approach to the play by providing new materials, characters or problems. For example: if the children are playing in a 'restaurant', the teacher may offer some costumes (for example: a chef's hat, or a handbag for the customer, to help define the role), suggest a challenge (for example: the customer is now in a hurry, the waiter is forgetful, the chef burns all the food), or even record the children improvising (using a video camera or iPad) so the children can watch and observe themselves at play. On the other hand, interrupting children during free dramatic play can create problems. You may discover that instead of extending and enriching the play, your intervention irrevocably changes, or even ends, it. You may unwittingly rob the children of an opportunity to discover something for themselves. It therefore becomes a question of knowing not only whether to intervene, but how and when.

Drama Lessons

While most early childhood centres provide opportunities for pretend play (such as the home corner, a dress-up box or a supermarket), drama lessons are a planned and purposeful time for drama and not a spontaneous moment that happens during your day. It will validate the importance of drama education and send a message to the children, your colleagues and the parent community that drama is respected, valued and important.

It will be beneficial for the children and their development, and also for your own development as an educator if you take some time to reflect on your practice and record how the lessons went. What would you do differently? What worked or didn't work? Remember, children at this age love repetition, so don't be afraid to offer the same lesson within a short period of time. Repeat it with your changes and record what happens. As you develop and practise the material, you become more comfortable and your confidence will increase.

Non-participation

Young children instinctively understand the concepts of pretending and make-believe, and most will eagerly participate in your drama class. But there may be one or two members of your class who prefer to sit out and watch. These children must be gently encouraged, but never forced to participate. It may take a few months for them to feel ready to join in. If possible, use an assistant or another adult in the room to sit with them. Don't allow them to wander off and play elsewhere in the classroom, but ask them to sit and observe their peers at work. You may find that the child is contributing when the group is working as a whole, but becomes hesitant when they are working in pairs or asked to do something on their own. Be sensitive to their needs and slowly help to build their self-confidence through small steps. Perhaps they might like to hold a costume or a prop rather than trying it on or using it. You might like to give them a musical instrument and ask them to create some sounds for a particular scene. You may want to consider using puppets and teaching puppetry skills. This is a wonderful way of introducing dramatic elements in a non-threatening way. Children who are reluctant to perform in front of peers will feel safer knowing that it is their puppet who is speaking and improvising, not them, as the audience's attention will be on the puppet rather than the child. It is important to remember that children who observe a drama class are still learning valuable skills. Allow them time and it is highly likely that they will eventually join in.

Preparation

The Space
Try to clear away as many distractions as possible. Drape or pin up material over toy shelves, move any furniture out of the way. A carpeted space is ideal, since many activities require the children to be on the floor. For large groups you will need a space that allows all the children to move about freely, without bumping into one another.

Class Size
Teachers who are beginning to incorporate drama into their curriculum must consider the group size. It is important that your space isn't too large – if it is, you risk losing control of the class. For younger children (3–4-year-olds) the ideal would be to split your class into smaller groups. If you can, try to teach one group while the other is outside with an assistant, or in another room. I appreciate that this is not always possible. For older children (5–8-year-olds) in a school setting, class size is important and you will need to establish clear guidelines. You may need to split the children into two groups for some activities, one group watching as the 'audience' and the other group 'performing'. Be conscious of allowing time for the groups to swap over. As you become more confident teaching drama, you will

find working with the whole class becomes more manageable and enjoyable.

Timing
This is purely up to you as a teacher and will depend on a number of factors. Generally, younger children can easily stay focused for 15–20 minutes of drama, which can be extended to 20–30 minutes as it becomes more familiar. Older children can sustain their attention for 30–60 minutes. But, of course, there is no hard-and-fast rule, and factors such as time of the day, group size, time of the school year, the weather and your energy levels all contribute to the length of the class.

The Freeze Rule
Establish this right from the beginning. When the teacher calls 'freeze', the children must learn to stop, look and listen. This will allow the teacher to give the class more instructions, keep the children physically safe and maintain control. Use the freeze rule in every class. You may also like to introduce an instrument for your freeze rule as a variation. Insist that the children do not touch anyone else in the room unless they are instructed to do so. See pages 2–3 for more detail on this technique.

Focus
I always begin every class with the children holding hands in a circle. It brings focus, readiness and a sense of celebration to each class. As the children enter, ask them to remove their shoes and sit in a circle. (It's also fine to leave shoes on, and may be easier for younger children.) Once the last child has joined the circle, invite the children to stand and hold hands. Ask them to take little steps forward into the centre of the circle (no running) and then big steps backwards. Insist that there is no pulling, running or falling down. Repeat this three or four times. Your class is now ready to enjoy drama. At the end of each lesson, I ask each child to stand tall and take a bow. Encourage them to try bowing as different characters, using different emotions, at different speeds and so forth. Finally, everyone claps and takes a final bow. This ensures that the children experience a sense of achievement, and helps to end the class on a positive note.

Costume/Props

Keep them simple. Too many items or costume pieces will distract the children from the learning. Either elect one item (such as a hat, a cape or a spoon) per child, or remove the costume/props altogether and rely instead on the children's acting (facial expressions, body language, vocal work) to show character, and their mime to show action (such as pretending to eat with a spoon).

Tips for Success

- Be enthusiastic! Participate fully in the lesson, rather than just giving instructions.

- Be prepared to 'role-play'. In some of these lessons you may need to pretend to be a character – a ringmaster, a bus driver, a waitress or a pirate captain. This will come naturally to some teachers, but others may find role-playing takes them out of their comfort zone. You might like to put on a piece of costume (such as a hat, a cape or some glasses) to help you get into character. Start small – try it out with just a few children and increase the group size until you feel confident to role-play in front of the whole class. Take a deep breath, put a smile on your face and go for it. You will find the children's response will be extremely positive and, like anything else, the more you practise, the better you will get.

- Continually move around the space – don't stand in one spot. It may be best if you and the children remove your shoes so you all feel comfortable and ready to create. Stand in the corner of the mat, in the centre of the room, crouch down and gather the children around you. Drama is always very physical, so be mentally and physically prepared.

- Keep your voice interesting. Use a variety of tones and expressions as you teach. Shout out loud, whisper 'secrets', attempt an accent or use pauses and gestures to create interest.

- Practise, practise, practise and play with new ideas. A great way to practise is to read picture books out loud to the class. Play with different expressions, volumes, intonations and accents. Be sure to try out different voices for each of the characters in the story. Please remember to take care of yourself and your voice. Teaching can become exhausting if you are continually raising your voice to gain the children's attention. Record and reflect upon your practice and be sure to take note of what techniques work best for you.

- Drama is noisy. Be prepared for all the children to be talking at once. This is fine, as long as you have established some simple rules to bring their attention back. You may use the freeze rule, which is explained on pages 2–3. Or, you may use an instrument (a bell or drum) or use a gesture (hands in the air, hands on your heads). But generally, each lesson has the children moving or making sound as a chorus (all together) so get ready to shut the doors and warn the nearby classrooms!

- Most importantly, relax and have fun! Drama has the ability to teach invaluable life skills and I believe it is essential in a child's education, but don't forget that drama is fun. Children are enjoying the experience while they are learning and developing skills. So relax… be prepared for a bit of chaos – and smile along the way. The children will appreciate it and your drama class will be a huge success. Enjoy!

Katherine Zachest

A Note on the Lesson Structure

You'll see that each lesson follows the same structure and I've included extension exercises for the older/more advanced students, as well as extracurricular activities for lessons outside the drama classroom.

Let's Get Started!

This lesson helps to establish dramatic rules and conventions – including the freeze rule and the importance of discussion – and helps the children to understand the way a drama class runs. I'd recommend you start with this lesson. Children explore using their body and voices to express emotions.

Resources
• Music to dance to.

WARM-UP
Warm-up Circle

Make a circle with the children holding hands. Let the children know that they should not fall over, pull anyone's arms or run. Once the students have formed a circle, proceed as follows:

- *Let's take little steps in, in, in. Look how small our circle is!*
- *Let's take big steps back, back, back. Look at how big our circle is!*
- *Remember, don't pull our friend's arms.*
- *Let's take little steps in, in, in. Let's say 'hello'.*
- *Let's take big steps back, back, back.*
- *One more time, coming in, in, in. Hello!*
- *And back, back, back.*
- *Let's let go of each other's hands.*
- *Stretch up as tall as you can.*
- *And now move down as small as you can.*
- *And now can you make yourself stretch out wide. Stretch your fingers out as well and reach to either side of the room.*
- *Good, and now can you cross your arms and give yourself a big hug? Squeeze tightly.*

The Freeze Rule

Ask the children to remain standing in a circle. Once the children are settled, proceed as follows:

- *I'm going to see how clever you are at being a statue.*
- *In a moment, I will ask you to wiggle your whole body, but when I call 'freeze', you have to be as still and as quiet as a statue.*
- *Ready? GO!*

Allow the children to wiggle their bodies for a count of five.

- *Freeze! Wow, look at these amazing statues. But I think I saw a little wiggle over here. Let's try again, ready, GO!*

Allow the children to move again.

- *Freeze! Wow, I can't believe how still you are. You are all very good at this.*

- *I am going to have to make it harder for you. This time let's walk around the space. We are going to stay on this mat (or another designated area, but keep it small so you maintain control and focus of the children).*

- *As you are moving around, there is no running and no touching anybody else. Be ready to freeze.*

Allow the children five counts to move around before calling 'freeze'. Compliment good statues and no sound.

- *Good, walking around again. This time when you freeze, can you freeze with your hands on your hips? Ready? Freeze.*

- *Good, walking around again. Now this time when you freeze can you put your arms in the air?*

Continue to get the children walking around and freezing in a specific statue. As they are walking, ask them to freeze as:

- o a tall giraffe
- o an apple with a stalk
- o a bird with large wings
- o a round ball
- o a tree with big branches
- o a cheeky monkey

You may also ask them to move differently. For example: they could try moving sideways, taking little or long steps, walking on tippy-toes or like a penguin.

Emotions

Ask the children to stand in a circle. When the children are settled, use the following instructions:

- *Show me your hands. Let's see if you can make your hands move in different ways.*
- *Can you make them move quickly?*
- *Can you make them move slowly?*
- *Can you make them look happy? (The hand 'bounces'.)*
- *Good, now let's make them look angry. (Tense, small shakes.)*
- *Good work, can you make them look shy? (Moves towards or behind the body.)*
- *And now let's make them look excited. (Moves quickly.)*
- *We can make our hands look different. Now let's try and make our bodies look different.*
- *Can you show me an angry statue? Good, now let's move around like we are angry. Remember, no running or touching anybody else. We are just pretending to be angry. Show me hands on hips. Show me crossing your arms. Make your hands look angry, angry arms, angry feet. I am going to ask you to freeze as an angry statue.*
- *Ready? Freeze. Can you say, 'I'm angry'? Excellent work.*
- *Take a big breath in and shake that one away.*
- *Now let's see if we can pretend to be sad. Show me sad shoulders, sad arms, sad back, sad knees and even sad feet. We are going to make a sad statue.*
- *Ready? Freeze. Can you say, 'I'm sad, boohoo'?*
- *And take a big breath in and blow that one away. Fantastic.*
- *Now let's imagine we are confused. Show me your thinking face. Can you scratch your head? Walk around and then change direction. You are very confused. We are going to freeze in a confused statue.*

- *Ready? Freeze. Can you say, 'I'm confused'?*
- *Good work, take a big breath in and blow that one away.*

Continue exploring different emotions, such as excitement, boredom and fear.

Discuss

Ask the children to sit in a circle. When the children are settled, ask them to discuss what they know about drama. You may like to use the following to guide the discussion:

- *Today we are going to do drama.*
- *Have you heard that word before?*
- *Do you know what it means?*

Allow the children some time to have a guess.

- *Drama is all about pretending and playing make-believe. In drama, we can pretend to be somebody or something else. And I know that you are already very good at drama. In fact, you have all just been doing drama now.*

Changing Your Voice

Ask the children to sit in a circle. When they are settled, proceed as follows:

- *You have all shown how you can change your face and your body to show different emotions. In drama, we also use our voices to play different characters. Now let's see what you can do with your voices.*
- *First, let's say 'good morning' in our normal voices.*
- *Now say 'good morning' like you are:*
  - o *scared*
  - o *sleepy*
  - o *angry*
  - o *excited*

5

- o *an old lady*
- o *a robot*
- o *telling a secret*
- o *a very important king*
- o *a pirate*
- o *a tiny little fairy*

Character

Ask the children to find their own place in the room. Remind them that there is no running and there is no touching anybody else. When the children are settled use the following instructions:

- *I am going to see if you can play some different characters. In drama, when we are acting different characters, we need to change our faces, we need to change our bodies and we need to change our voices. Let's try a few different characters.*

- *When I call 'freeze', I am going to get you to show me a frozen statue of that character. Let's begin by walking around as yourself.*

Read the following instructions in a witch's voice.

- *Now as you are walking imagine you are becoming a wicked old witch. Can you curl up your spine, curl your fingers and bring your elbows out? Can you wrinkle up your face? Now let's cackle like a witch. Walk around looking for something for your secret potion. Bend down and show me you are holding something disgusting. Put it in your cauldron and stir. Let out a big cackle again. And freeze!*

Read the following instructions in your regular voice.

- *Good, take a big breath and blow that one away. Return to your natural walk.*

- *Now as you are moving around, imagine you are becoming a king or a queen.*

Read the following instructions in a regal voice.

- *Put on your royal cloak and place your crown on your head. You are very important. Put your nose up in the air. Take strong, careful, royal steps. Show me your fancy fingers as you walk. Can you say, 'How do you do?' And freeze!*

Read the following instructions in your regular voice.

- *Good, let's take in a big breath and blow that one away. Return to your natural walk.*

- *And now, finally, as you are moving can you imagine you are becoming a robot?*

Read the following instructions in a robot's voice.

- *Make your movements stiff and jerky. Straighten up your spine. Show me your robot arms moving at your side. Robots, can you look down? Robots, can you look up? Can you look side to side? Can you say in your robot voice, 'I am a robot'? And freeze!*

- *Excellent work, take a big breath and blow that one away.*

Mime

Ask the children to stand and find a place in front of you. Remind them that during this next activity, there is no touching anybody else. When the children are settled use the following instructions:

- *Sometimes in drama, we use mime. Have you heard that word before? Do you know what it means? Mime means that we are acting without making a sound. We use our faces and our bodies to communicate, but we turn our voices off. We will be doing lots of mime activities when we are doing drama. You have already shown me that you are very clever at miming. Let's try some more.*

- *Can you mime holding a ball? Let's mime throwing it up and catching it. Good, follow the ball with your eyes. Now can you mime bouncing the ball? Good, now can you mime throwing the ball as far as you can?*

- *Now can you mime holding an apple? Good, now let's mime taking a bite of the apple. Fill up your cheeks and pretend to chew. Can you mime swallowing the apple? Good, now throw the apple away!*

- *Now can you mime patting a dog? Show me how big or small the dog is. Good, remember, mime is no sound.*

- *Let's try miming having a big laugh. Who can show me a big laugh without making any sound? Excellent!*

- *Can you mime picking up a little baby chick? Now carefully carry the chick and put it in a nest.*

Continue with more miming actions. Try to keep the actions within the children's experience. Think of things that they do every day. For example: brushing their hair, brushing their teeth, drawing a picture or eating with a spoon.

Discuss

Ask the children to sit in a circle. Congratulate them on all the work they have done in drama. Compliment the children for trying something new, for showing good miming technique, for good use of their voice or for good acting.

Musical Statues

It is very likely that you have played this with your class before, but it is a fun way to finish and reinforces the idea of the freeze rule. Do not play for elimination. Instead ask them to dance as different emotions or characters. Play some dancing music. Ask the children to move or dance around the space. When the music stops, the children must freeze. Try getting them to freeze in different kinds of statues. Use some of the ideas that they have explored during the class.

FINISH

Ask the children to stand in a circle. When the children are settled, use the following instructions:

- *Can you stand tall?*
- *Can you take a bow?*
- *Give yourself a round of applause!*

LET'S GET STARTED!

ONE

BUILDING ON IMAGINATION

The Enchanted Forest

Resources

- A tambourine or any instrument that rattles or shakes.

- Some gentle, light music to be played in the background during the narration.

- Three large pieces of fabric in different colours and textures (optional).

- Simple costume ideas for fairies, elves and giants as suggested in *Focus* (optional).

WARM-UP
The Circle

Make a circle with the children holding hands. Remind the children that they cannot fall over, pull anyone's arms or run. Once the children have formed a circle use the following instructions:

- *Let's take little steps in, in, in. Look how small our circle is!*
- *Let's take big steps back, back, back. Look at how big our circle is!*
- *Let's take little steps in, in, in. Let's say 'hello'.*
- *Let's take big steps back, back, back. Let's let go of each other's hands.*
- *Let's make ourselves as big as we can. Stretch out your legs. Stretch up your arms. Look at how big you are! You look like giants!*
- *Let's make ourselves as small as we can. Look how small you are! I can hardly see you!*
- *Let's make ourselves as flat as we can. How flat can you be?*
- *Let's make ourselves round. Big round arms. Big round backs. You look like big round balls!*
- *Let's make ourselves as wide as we can. Stretch your hands out to the side. Stand with your legs stretched out.*

Making a Magical Forest

Inform the children that you are now going to make a magical forest. Ask the children to find a space on their own.

- *Can you get down as small as you can?*
- *When I make this sound, can you slowly grow bigger and bigger? Ready?*

Shake the tambourine.

- *Let's slowly grow into a tree. Stretch up your arms. Reach up your fingers like the leaves on a tree.*

Sway your arms in the air, imagining there is a gentle breeze. You are all wonderful, magical trees.

- *Let's get down again to a tiny seed. Slowly let's shrink down as small as you can.*

Ask the children to sit where they are and to listen to the story you will tell them. Narrate the following as you play some gentle music softly in the background.

- *Once upon a time, in a land far away, there were tiny seeds waiting under the earth. But these weren't ordinary seeds; they were magical, enchanted seeds.*

Shake the tambourine.

- *And one day when the sun shone down, the seeds began to grow. They grew… and they grew… and they grew…*

Shake the tambourine.

- *Their branches reached out far and wide. And when the wind blew through the forest, the trees swayed and danced in the wind.*

Shake the tambourine.

- *In this enchanted forest there lived many wonderful and magical creatures. There were the tiny little fairies. Let's all turn ourselves into the fairies now.*

Fairies

Ask the children to stand and walk around the space and proceed as follows:

- *As you are walking around the room imagine you are getting lighter. Imagine you are so light that you are floating. Make your steps as light and soft as you can.*
- *Walk on your tippy-toes as you float around the room.*
- *Imagine you have wings. Fly around the room with your magical fairy wings. Fly gracefully around the room. Freeze as a flying fairy statue.*
- *This is your magical flying fairy. Can you remember your magical flying fairy?*

15

- *And in the magical enchanted forest, there also lived the elves. Let's turn ourselves into elves now.*

Elves

- *Let's walk around the room. Can you take tiny little steps? Can you make your steps faster?*
- *Show me your elf hiding behind a rock.*
- *Now can you show me how your elf moves to hide behind a tree?*
- *Join with another elf. Can you find a way to scurry together?*
- *Can you show me a cheeky face?*
- *How do elves sound when they giggle? Can you show me your elf giggle?*
- *This is your elf. Can you remember your elf?*
- *And in the magical enchanted forest, there also lived the giants. Let's turn ourselves into giants now.*

Giants

- *Let's walk around the room.*
- *Make your arms grow bigger. Make your legs grow bigger. Make your back grow longer. Make your head get bigger.*
- *Can you take big, slow, heavy steps?*
- *Can you make your body big and tall and strong?*
- *Can you make your voice sound big? Let's all say, 'Get out of my way!'*
- *This is your giant. Can you remember your giant?*

FOCUS

Divide the space into three areas – one for the fairies, one for the elves and one for the giants. Lay down the three pieces of fabric around the central performance space and nominate a group for each piece as you lay it. Select children to sit on the pieces of fabric and to be the fairies, giants or elves. Explain to the children they will have a chance to play the other characters later.

It is optional to provide each student with a costume. If you do, keep them very simple so they can be put on and taken off quickly. Choose one item such as:

- o Fairies: fairy wings, a wand, a strip of fabric tied around the waist, a tiara or a crown
- o Elves: a 'Santa' or elf hat, a vest, a strip of fabric around the waist or a scarf
- o Giants: Wellington boots, a vest or jacket, a hat or a square of fabric tied as a cape

Begin with all the children 'asleep' on their piece of fabric. Narrate the story 'The Enchanted Forest' and encourage the children to enter the performance space and engage with the story before returning to their original spot. Encourage vocal participation in chorus, where the children talk at the same time. For example: all the fairies might say together, 'We are the fairies of the enchanted forest.'

The Enchanted Forest Story

- *Once upon a time, there was an enchanted forest. The enchanted forest began as tiny seeds under the ground. After many sunny days and plenty of soft rain, the seeds sprouted and began to grow and grow and grow.*

Use the tambourine to indicate that all the children should go into the performance space and grow into a forest.

- *But this forest wasn't an ordinary forest; it was filled with wonderful creatures.*

Use the tambourine to indicate that the children should return to their original spot.

- *There were the beautiful and enchanting fairies that flew around the forest.*

Use the tambourine to indicate that the fairies fly around space; or you may wish to use music as the fairies do this.

> NARRATOR: We are the fairies of the enchanted forest.
>
> FAIRIES: We are the fairies of the enchanted forest.

Use the tambourine to indicate that the fairies return to their original spot.

- *And there were also the sneaky elves who loved to play hide-and-seek.*

Use the tambourine or music to indicate that the elves move to centre.

> NARRATOR: We are the elves of the enchanted forest.
>
> ELVES: We are the elves of the enchanted forest.

Use the tambourine to indicate that the elves return to their original spot.

- *And then there were the gentle giants who stomped through the forest with great big steps.*

Use the tambourine or music to indicate that the giants move to centre.

> NARRATOR: We are the giants of the enchanted forest.
>
> GIANTS: We are the giants of the enchanted forest.

Use the tambourine to indicate that the giants return to their spot.

When narrating the following section, ask the children for suggestions, and use them either as a chorus or individually.

- *Sometimes the characters of the enchanted forest would make a big pot of their favourite, magic soup. The fairies came to the middle of the forest. They had been busy all day collecting some_____ and when they came to the pot they put in some_____. Then the fairies went back to their little flower house.*

- *The elves scurried around in the forest collecting more ingredients and when they came to the pot, they put in some _____. Then the elves went back to their little house at the bottom of the trees.*

- *Then the giants stomped through the forest. They reached up high and stretched down low collecting more ingredients. Then the giants stomped to the pot and put in some _____.*

- *Then all the creatures from the enchanted forest would make a circle and dance around the pot singing 'Bubble Bubble Soup'.*

Extend the song for older children. Find ways of building the song using rhyming and chants. Encourage input and ideas from the children.

- *When they had finished, they all sat down and enjoyed a delicious bowl of enchanted forest soup.*

Children mime eating the soup.

- *They waved goodbye to each other and returned to their houses to sleep. And that was the end of the story.*

- *Can you all stand up and take a bow? Now give yourselves a big clap.*

- *Everyone return to your original spot. Take off your costume. Put it down carefully where you were sitting. Now, everyone, we are going to have a turn at being a different character. I'm going to explain to you which character you will be next.*

Move the children in a clockwise direction to their new fabric and character.

- *Put on your new costume. Let's explore the enchanted forest again.*

Repeat the story after the children have swapped characters and costumes. You might like to change the ingredients or the words of the song. Remember to use the children's ideas and suggestions as you narrate.

FINISH
Forest Freeze

Place the three pieces of fabric around the space and allocate each one a character, for example: this is for the fairy, this is for the elf and this is for the giant. Once the children know which piece of fabric represents which character, start the following activity:

- Play some music. Ask the children to move and dance about the space while it is playing. Stop the music and call out a character. The children must quickly move to the appropriate piece of fabric and freeze in that character.

- Play the music again. The children leave the fabric and begin moving around the space until the music stops and the next character is called out. Repeat.

Extension

For older children, extend the movement sequence around the pot.

For example: you could narrate: circle left, circle right, move in, move out, clap your hands three times.

Encourage the children to create a simple chant in their groups using rhymes. For example:

> We are the Fairies
> Small and light
> We can fly
> Through day and night.

Select some children to take it in turns to be the narrator.

Ask the characters to interact with each other during the story to encourage improvisation.

Extracurricular Activities

- Make a magic wand.
- Draw a picture of your favourite character.

- Make a forest mural with the whole class.
- Sprinkle glitter outside to make your own enchanted forest.
- Go on an excursion to a local forest, parkland or some public gardens.
- Have a fairy and elf party (teachers as giants!).
- Make some soup – real or imagined, using things from nature.
- Read books about fairies, elves or giants.

The Magic Carpet

Resources

- A box, bag or basket with a square scarf or small piece of fabric for each child.
- Relaxation music.

WARM-UP
The Circle

Begin with 'The Circle' (see *The Enchanted Forest*, page 14).

Hot Sand

Ask the children to start moving in all directions around the space. Insist on no running, touching or making sound. Use the freeze rule. As children engage in the activity make sure you compliment good statues. After 2–3 minutes, ask the children to move as if they are:

o walking on hot sand
o moving through cold water
o walking on sticky honey
o walking in gooey mud
o walking in a dark forest
o walking on wobbly jelly

Copy Cat

Ask the children to sit in a circle. Make lots of different sounds and ask the children to copy each sound as you make it. Try to use a wide variety of sounds, for example: sounds that are quick, slow, high, low, soft and loud. You might also like to use some of the children's suggestions. For example, use:

o zzzzz
o shhh
o pop pop pop
o la la la la
o bing bong
o ch ch ch
o bam bam bam
o ding ding ding
o wooooooo

Discuss

Ask the children the following questions:

- *Have you been on a holiday?*
- *Where did you go?*
- *How did you get there?*
- *What did you see?*

Tell the children that today we are going on a holiday to lots of different places. Ask the children to guess how they are going to travel. After listening to several responses tell them they are going to travel on their very own magic carpet.

Ask the children to sit in a circle. Hold the basket with the scarves and explain to the children that inside are magic carpets waiting to fly them somewhere special. Hand out a carpet to each child. Ask the children to spread out their carpet and sit on it. Continue until all of the children are seated. Ensure that you have a carpet as well.

If you do not have a square of fabric for each child, you could use one large tablecloth or bedspread and all sit together.

FOCUS

Read the following with the children:

- *Oh no, I've noticed we aren't flying. Why aren't we flying? We forgot to put the magic in. Can you clap three times?*

- *Now rub your hands together as fast as you can. Can you feel your hands tingling? This is the magic.*

- *Hold the magic over your carpet.*

- *But we still aren't flying! I remember now… we need to chant the magic words. Oh no! I've forgotten the magic words. Who knows what the magic words are?*

Use the children's ideas, either selecting one or combining a few, depending on the age group. For example: 'bippety bippety bop, carpet fly up' or 'zip zap zoom, abracadabra'. For younger children, use just one word, for example: 'Abracadabra!' When the children have decided on the magic word, read the following:

- *Whoa! Here we go. Hold on tight.*

- *Fly this way (lean to the left).*

- *Now around this cloud (lean to the right).*

- *We're going over a big rain cloud (lean back).*

- *Look! There are some birds flying around us.*

- *How fast can we go? How high can we go?*

- *Oh no! We don't know how to make this carpet land. Who can remember the magic words to make us land? Can everyone share what you think the magic words are?*

Again, use the children's ideas to create the magic word. Either select one idea or combine a few ideas, depending on the age group of the children. for example: 'carpet down now' or use simple sounds such as 'shhh'.

- *Coming in for landing. Where are we? There's something sticky.*

- *Feel it with your fingers, your toes.*

- *Get some sticky and put it on your arms. Get some sticky and put it on your legs. Get some sticky and put it on your tummy. Can you put some on your back… your hair… your face?*

- *Now let's walk around.*
- *We must be in sticky land!*

Explore the world with an emphasis on movement. You may want to play some music in the background. Ask the children the following:

- *Imagine you are stuck together as you move.*
- *Imagine you have one foot stuck to the ground.*
- *Imagine you have to climb a sticky mountain and cross a sticky creek.*
- *It is time to go!*
- *Wash the sticky off* (mime showering).
- *Come back to your magic carpet and sit down. Say our magic words for take-off on the count of three: 1, 2, 3 and* _____
- *Try flying while we are standing up on our carpets. Try flying while we are balancing on one leg.*
- *Look over the side of our carpet. Time for landing.*

Explore numerous different lands, either using the children's suggestions or your own examples. Examples of different lands you could try include:

- o fast land
- o balloon land
- o monster land
- o lolly land
- o robot land
- o sleepy land
- o slow land
- o water land

Explore each land and then return to the magic carpets. To finish the activity, explain to the children that you have been gone for a long time and they have to return to school. As you fly back to the school you will pass back over the lands you have been exploring. Name each land as you pass by. Wave goodbye as you name each land. Fly back to the room you started in. Ask the children to lie on their carpets with their eyes closed. Once they are doing so, remind them of their adventures, pausing after you name each land.

As you go through each land, remind the children how they moved, what they saw, ate, touched and so on. You may choose to use relaxation music while the children visualise each land.

FINISH

Ask the children which land they enjoyed going to and why. What did you like about _____ land? Why? What did it remind you of?

Ask the children to stand up and scrunch their carpet very small. Ask them to throw their carpet in the air and try to catch it. Repeat three times. Finally, ask them to scrunch their fabric and whisper 'thank you, magic carpet' before returning it into the box or bag. Ask the children to stand tall and take a bow, then give themselves a round of applause.

Extension

Divide children into pairs or small groups and ask them to come up with a small scene where they discover the magic carpet, use a magic chant, fly to a new land, encounter a problem, solve the problem and return 'home'.

Use this class to explore different countries or environments. Divide the class into small groups and give each group a country and ask them to improvise a small scene using their knowledge of that region. Or ask them to land in a desert, a forest, a beach or a mountain.

Explore planets of the solar system. Ask children to research conditions on the planets and improvise a scene about landing on the planet.

Extracurricular Activities

- Use paper weaving to make a carpet.
- Discuss the way fabric is made around the world.
- Draw or paint a picture of your favourite land.
- Go on magic-carpet rides outside. Name parts of the playground as different lands, for example: the hill becomes bouncing land, the sandpit is the desert.
- Have a picnic on the magic carpets and eat magic food.

- Ask the children to share their own magic carpet adventure, or write their own story.
- Peg the carpets together and hang them across the room or make a magic-carpet pathway.

Pirates

Resources

- A headscarf for each child.
- Eye patches (optional).
- A pirate hat or headscarf for the teacher in role as pirate captain.
- Chairs, mats or cushions to build a boat, or use rope or chalk (optional).

WARM-UP

Emotions

Ask the children to run on the spot. Use the freeze rule. After 1–2 minutes, ask the children to complete the following:

- *Stretch up tall.*
- *Bend down and touch your toes.*
- *Stand up tall.*
- *Reach to the right.*
- *Stand up tall.*
- *Reach to the left.*

Ask the children to show you a statue from the following list of emotions. Remind them to use their face and body when creating the statue. You may want to bring the statues to 'life' by moving around the space and giving the children a simple line to repeat, for example: 'I'm so happy.' You can also use:

- o sad
- o excited
- o scared
- o tired
- o confused
- o bored
- o scary
- o shy
- o grumpy

Grumpy Pirates

Ask the children to continue being grumpy and to transform into pirates. Ask them to say the following:

- o Arrrghhh!
- o Get out of my way.
- o Ahoy there!
- o Arghh, me hearty.

Discuss

Sit the children in a circle and ask a series of questions to gauge their understanding of pirates.

- *What do you know about pirates?*
- *What do they do?*
- *What do they look like?*
- *How do they get around?*
- *What do they do with treasure once they find it?*

FOCUS

Tie a headscarf to each child or help the children to tie their own. Ask the children to practise their pirate walk, talk and faces. If you use eye patches, suggest the children wear them on their foreheads as it can be disorienting to wear them over the eye for long periods.

Play the role of the pirate captain. Being in role helps you to maintain the focus and control of the class, guide the improvisation and engage the children. Use a pirate hat if possible, or tie on a headscarf. Build a boat with the class by placing chairs, small mats or cushions in a circle. You could also mark a circle with rope, or chalk, or designate an area on the mat to become the boat. Once you have become the pirate captain, put on your hat or headscarf and speak in a pirate voice. If and when you need to step out of role, remove the hat or headscarf first. Begin with the following sequence:

• *Salute the captain.*

The children stand still and salute.

• *Scrub the deck.*

The children mime scrubbing the deck on all fours.

• *Climb the rigging.*

The children mime climbing.

• *Hoist the sails.*

The children mime pulling on ropes.

• *Land ahoy!*

The children mime looking through a telescope.

The Pirate-Ship Story

As you call out the following orders, in the role of captain, ask the children to respond with 'Aye Aye Captain'. You may want to remove your hat or headscarf when you step out of role. Use the children's ideas to build the story:

CAPTAIN: Okay, pirates, we are off on a journey to find treasure. Are you all ready?

CHILDREN: Aye aye, Captain!

CAPTAIN: This ship is a mess. Scrub the deck! Climb the rigging! Salute the captain!

CHILDREN: Aye aye, Captain!

CAPTAIN: Here we go on a new adventure. We're off to find treasure.

TEACHER: Can you move your body from side to side as we rock inside the pirate ship?

CAPTAIN: Now get out your telescopes. Who can see an island? Where? What is the island called? What dangers are there on _____ Island? Well, I have heard that there is also treasure on the island. I once stole some treasure, many, many years ago. And it looks like this.

Hold out your hands. Build the illusion by carefully showing the 'treasure' around the circle. Don't let the children touch or grab at your hands. Then carefully mime putting the treasure in your pocket.

CAPTAIN: I will stay on board to guard the ship. The rest of you pirates go to the island and try to find some treasure. But beware of the

_____.

Children swim over to the island and return with their treasure. Allow them to explore their role-playing freely. This may take some children longer than others, so encourage them back to the ship by preparing to set sail. Once the students are back on the boat complete the following:

- *Can you all show me your treasure?*

- *Let's put the treasure away in our treasure chests.*

Mime the following actions:

- *Let's get out our keys and unlock the treasure chest.*

- *Let's open the lid.*

- *Carefully put the treasure inside.*

- *Close the lid and lock the treasure box.*

- *Let's put our treasure boxes away and put your key in a safe place.*

Repeat this activity going to different islands, selecting different children to tell you the name of the island and the possible dangers (sharks, monsters, giant crabs, a scary octopus, mermaids).

You will be able to control the group if you remain in role and shout out orders. While 'at sea' the pirates can:

o drink some pirate punch
o make up some songs and sea shanties
o make and eat 'pirate stew'
o get seasick and mime vomiting overboard

Continue to be guided by the children's ideas and suggestions and gently bring the focus back to you as the pirate captain. You may like to pretend that there is a man overboard, that sharks are attacking the boat or that you are caught in a giant storm. When things get noisy and a little out of control, repeat the orders from the focus activity. If necessary, come out of role to facilitate classroom management.

FINISH
What Will You Do with Your Treasure?

Sail back to school. Open your treasure boxes. Admire each other's treasure. Go around the circle and ask each child:

* *What have you got?*
* *What will you do with your treasure?*

Pirate's (or King's) Treasure

* Line the children along one end of the room.
* Stand at the other end of the room, facing away from the children.
* Explain that you are the pirate.
* Place a 'treasure' behind you at your feet.
* The children must slowly creep up towards the treasure.
* Every time you turn around to face the children they must freeze.
* If you see anybody moving, send them back to the start.
* If a child gets the treasure, they must quickly move back to their starting position.
* That child becomes the next 'pirate'.

Extension

Divide the children into groups of 3 or 4. Ask them to create a simple scene titled 'Adventure on Skull Island'. They might want to use mime, the role of narrator, object transformation (see lessons on pages 85–93 and 95–102) or any other dramatic convention that they know. It is a good idea to remind the children to keep the scene simple. The scene should also have a clear beginning (the pirates at sea), middle (the pirates dig up the treasure and are chased by the sea monsters), and an end (the pirates defeat the sea monsters and return to their ship).

Extracurricular Activities

- Read some books about pirates.
- Make a treasure box.
- Draw or paint a picture from your adventure.
- Organise a treasure hunt (indoors or outdoors). Use rocks, beads, feathers and 'gold' coins.
- Walk the plank – set up a balancing activity using boards, a rope or draw a line with chalk.
- Hide 'treasure' in the sandpit.
- Make a simple boat using a plastic container decorated with stickers. Set sail in a larger container or tank of water and get the children to create a storm by blowing through a straw.
- Explore things that float, things that sink.
- Have a pirate party and encourage the children to dress up.

Robots

Resources

- 'The Dingle Dangle Scarecrow'.
- Some music that suits the theme of 'robots', perhaps an instrumental piece with a fast tempo and hard beats such as techno or industrial.
- 'Heads, Shoulders, Knees and Toes' (optional).

ROBOTS

WARM-UP
Strong and Soft

Begin by standing in a circle. Ask the children to alternate between strong and soft positions. When you ask the children to be strong, use a loud and purposeful voice, when you ask them to be soft, use a gentle, quiet voice. Use instruments such as a drum (strong) and xylophone (soft) as the children make their positions. After 3–4 minutes of making strong and soft positions, use the following instructions:

- *Can you make yourself very straight?*
- *Can you make your arms stiff by your side? Can you make your legs stiff and straight?*
- *Can you make your bodies strong? Shoulders back, chin in.*
- *Take a deep breath in. As you breathe out... Can you relax your face? Can you let your shoulders drop? Can you let your knees bend?*
- *Can you flop around in a flippy-floppy shape?*
- *Take another big breath in. As you breathe out... Let yourself melt down to the ground.*
- *Fall asleep on the floor and take big breaths in and out.*

Nursery Rhymes

Read 'The Dingle Dangle Scarecrow' to the children. Ask the children to begin by lying on the floor sleeping and then to mime the action in each stanza as you read through the nursery rhyme. Repeat the activity, inviting the children to say or sing the nursery rhyme with you.

Robots

Begin by asking the children to find their own place on the floor and lie down. Play the music softly underneath your narration. Take your time reading the narration to give the children time to explore and isolate each body part. When all the children are in position and the music is playing, read the following to the children:

- *Imagine you are pieces of metal: nuts and bolts. We are going to put all those pieces of metal together to build ourselves into a robot.*

- *Imagine your feet are building. Can you wiggle your toes?*

- *Your feet are connecting to your knees. Can you bend your knees?*

- *Can you make your robot body connect to the legs? Can you move so you are sitting up?*

- *Now let's build the shoulders, move your shoulders up and down. Let's attach the arms and the robot hands. Can you move your robot fingers?*

- *Lastly, the neck and the head. Can you move your head from side to side?*

- *Let's all stand up.*

- *Open your robot eyes. Can you open and shut them? Find a piece to put on your robot nose. Does it wiggle? Now find two more pieces to attach for your ears.*

- *The last piece is your robot mouth. Open and close your mouth.*

- *Now I am going to press the button that will bring you to life. When I turn you on, you can start moving around the space.*

Move around to each child pressing an imaginary button and make a 'beep' sound as you do. Let the children explore their new character and make the music louder. After a couple of minutes turn the music down (or off) and give the 'robots' the following orders, using a robotic voice:

- *Raise one arm.*

- *Raise the other arm.*

- *Balance on one leg.*

41

- *Take two steps forward.*
- *Take two steps backwards.*
- *Wave 'hello'.*
- *Eat and drink.*
- *Brush your teeth.*
- *Go to sleep.*

Now sing the following song together with the children in a slow and robotic voice. Ask the children to mime the action for each line of the nursery rhyme.

> When all the children were sleeping,
> And the moon behind the clouds,
> Up jumped the robot,
> And shouted very loud,
> I'm a stiff and jerky robot,
> With a very straight hat,
> I can move my hands like this,
> And move my feet like that.

Repeat the song allowing the children to sing along as they mime. Invite the children to sing along using a robotic voice. Once the children have had a chance to practise the song, tell them they are going to practise everyday jobs as a robot. Read the following to the children:

- *Now, robots, let's practise everyday jobs. Robots can you:*
  - *vacuum the carpet?*
  - *wash the dishes?*
  - *wash the car?*
  - *clean the windows?*
  - *make the beds?*
  - *wash the clothes?*
  - *hang out the washing?*
  - *cook the dinner?*
  - *wipe down the benches?*
  - *pick some flowers?*
  - *sweep the floors?*
  - *do some gardening?*
  - *paint the house?*
  - *do your homework?*
  - *clean the bathroom?*
  - *mend some clothes?*

FOCUS
A Robot Story

Read the following story to the children. Ask the children to mime the action of the story. Begin the story with the children asleep on the floor as the lazy child.

- *Once upon a time, there was a child who never wanted to do any chores. The child's mother and father were always asking the child to help with the many jobs around the house, but the child was lazy. So one day, the child decided to build a robot to take care of the jobs the child did not want to do. The child worked very hard. The child worked all day and all night, until finally one morning, the child had finished!*

Play robotic music.

- *Now, can you imagine you are the robot?*

Move around the children as they begin to 'build' into their robot character.

- *The child pressed the special buttons on each of the robots that brought them to life.*

The teacher in the role of child brings each robot to life by pressing the 'special button' on each 'robot' and saying 'beep'.

- *And then the robots were set off to work.*
- *Okay robots… off you go to work.*

Children come to life and mime the movements of the everyday jobs. The teacher gives the robots instructions to help the robots do the everyday jobs. Use ideas from the list above.

- *As the robots worked, the child rested under the shade of a favourite tree.*

Teacher in the role of child yawns and pretends to sleep.

- *But then, as child slept, something went wrong. Very wrong! The robots got faster and faster at their jobs. Faster and faster until finally they went into a crazy, out-of-control robot frenzy!*

Children continue to improvise as robots doing their chores but in fast-forward.

- *And then, with a big noise, the robots started to fall apart. Slowly, slowly, bit by bit, the robots fell apart until the robots were just a big pile of metal and nuts and bolts.*

Children make noise and then crumble slowly down to the floor. Stop the music.

- *Just then, the child's mother came in, and saw all the mess on the floor. She demanded the child clean up all this mess at once!*

The teacher is in role as the mother.

> MOTHER: What's all this mess? You need to clean this up right away.

- *Now the child had even more work to do. The child spent the rest of the day cleaning up the big mess. When the big mess was cleaned up, the child had to complete all the jobs around the house.*

Ask the children to take on the role of the child and mime cleaning up the mess.

- *And from that day on, the child always helped mother and father around the house. And that is the end of the story.*

- *Children, take a bow and give yourselves a round of applause.*

FINISH

Sing 'Heads, Shoulders, Knees and Toes' to help the students get out of role from being robots. Alternatively, reuse 'The Dingle Dangle Scarecrow' from the start of the lesson.

Extension

As the children create their robot, ask them to think of a name for it and tell the audience the job for which it was created. For example: 'I am B34Z, and I am a sweeping robot.'

Divide the class into small groups. Ask them to improvise a scene with at least one robot character. Groups must include a moment of fast-forward and/or a moment of slow motion. Encourage the children to face the audience, speak loudly and express themselves both physically and vocally.

Extracurricular Activities

• Discuss how robots and robotics are used today in manufacturing.

• Create a 'production line', by lining the children in a row and passing real or imagined objects down the line. For example: you might pass blocks down the line and the last person/people can build a tower using the blocks. Repeat the activity in reverse. Set it to music.

• Use a collection of boxes, aluminium foil and recycled materials to create your own robot.

• Write a story about your dream robot.

• Draw or paint a picture of a robot.

• Read books about inventions and how the use of robotics impacts the world.

The Royal Castle

Resources

- Costume items to represent a royal family for up to half the group.
- A dragon mask or a hat to represent a dragon (you can find great Chinese dragon heads in Chinese handicraft stores or online).
- A large piece of transparent fabric (optional).
- Royal-sounding music, such as trumpets and classical music.
- Little sequins or stars.

WARM-UP
Group Work

Ask the children to walk around the space. Ask the
students to freeze. Once in the freeze position, ask
the students to find a partner. With their partners,
the students make the following shapes using their
bodies:

o circle
o star
o dinosaur

Ask the children to walk around the space, then
freeze. Ask the students to form a group of 3 and
make the following shapes:

o jellyfish
o a hen with her eggs
o traffic lights

Ask the children to walk around the space, then
freeze. Ask the students to form a group of 4 or 5
and make the following shapes:

o house with a chimney
o bird on a nest
o bridge

Ask the children to walk around the space, then
freeze. Ask the students to form one big group and
make the following shapes:

o dragon
o forest
o castle

Kings, Queens, Princes and Princesses

Ask the students to stand in their own spot in the
space. Use the following instructions:

• *Let's all move around the space. Remember, no
running and or touching anybody else.*

• *When I call 'freeze', I need you to become still like
a statue. Ready? Freeze! Excellent statues.*

- Let's move around the space again. Freeze. Excellent statues.

- Let's move around the space again. Now as you are moving, I want you to imagine that you are a king. Put on your fancy cloak. Put on your golden crown. Put your nose into the air as you walk. Can you say 'How do you do?' in your king's voice? Freeze. Show me your statue of an important king. Excellent work.

- Let's shake that one away.

- Moving around the room again, I want you to imagine that you are the queen. Can you put on your fancy long gown? Put on your jewel-encrusted crown. Put on your rings and show me your fancy fingers as you walk. Can you say 'How do you do?' in your queen's voice? Freeze. Show me how the queen might stand. Fantastic.

- Let's shake that one away.

- Moving around the room again. Let's imagine we are the brave knights. Put on your silver armour. Put on your protective helmet. Make your shoulders bigger and wider as you walk. Show me your brave face. Can you say, 'I am the brave knight' in your knight's voice? Freeze. Show me your brave knight statue. Excellent.

- Shake that one away.

- Now find a place on your own and get down as small as you can.

Discuss

Inform the children that we are going to visit a castle. Ask the children what charracters live in a castle? Reinforce the characters of the castle by stating something along the lines of:

- That's right, kings, queens, princesses and princes are characters that live in a castle, along with royal knights to protect the palace.

FOCUS
Growing into a Dragon

Slowly count down from ten to one and ask the children to grow into a forest, using their arms as branches and their hands as leaves. Ask them to keep their bodies still, like thick, strong tree trunks. Narrate the story while the children are in the forest position. Move around the children as you speak:

- *Once upon a time, there was a large forest, with tall trees that stretched high into the sky. Some people believed that the trees were over one hundred years old. And in the centre of this ancient forest, there was a tall hill. Perched right on the top of the hill stood a wonderful castle.*

- *Can you move to the castle position all together? Excellent, hold that position nice and strong.*

- *The castle had strong walls made of stone and had high turrets around the walls. The castle had stood on the hill for as long as anyone could remember. Inside the castle there lived the royal family. Deep in the forest, inside a dark cave, there lived… a dragon.*

- *Come on everyone; let's become the dragon of the forest. I'm going to be the dragon's head; can you help me make the body? Join on behind me.*

- *The dragon moved slowly through the forest, towards the castle on the hill. And as it moved it let out a gigantic ROAR!*

- *Can you help me ROAR like the dragon! Excellent, now we are ready to tell the rest of the story.*

Meeting the Dragon

Divide the class into two groups. One group will be the royal family and the other will be the dragon. Alternatively, divide the class into three groups, the dragon, the royal family and the audience. Explain that you will swap them around later and everybody will have a turn at being the royal family or the dragon, including the audience.

Costume

Divide the royal family group into characters: king, queen, princesses, princes, royal servants and royal knights. Tie a scarf around each member of the royal family group as a cloak. Add other items if you wish, such as a crowns, tiaras, capes and vests. Remember to keep the costume items simple to avoid the children getting distracted.

Select one child to become the head of the dragon. You may wish to give them a mask or a hat. If you wish you can drape a large piece of transparent fabric over several children to make the dragon body. Ask the children to get underneath the fabric and hold on to it. Make sure they can all see.

Performance

To begin the performance, place the royal family into an offstage position on one side of the performance space. Place the dragon group offstage on the other side of the performance space. If you have an audience, seat them in front of the performance space.

Play the royal music as the royal family enters the space. Read the following story with the students adding mime and dialogue:

> NARRATOR: Ladies and gentleman, presenting the royal family!
>
> *Royal family group enter.*
>
> The royal family always bows or curtsies when they enter a room.
>
> *The royal family bows or curtsies.*
>
> The royal family always introduces themselves when they enter the space.
>
> *Each character says a simple opening line, for example: 'I am the king of the royal castle.'*
>
> One day, the royal family were all enjoying a lovely cup of tea and eating freshly baked scones with jam and cream, when they heard a terrible and frightening sound.
>
> *The dragon roars from offstage.*

They were all very frightened, even the brave knights. They began to quiver with fear.

Each of the royal family characters says a second line. For example: 'What was that?' 'Was that a volcano?' 'We're doomed!'

The sound got louder and louder. The royal family knew that whatever made the noise, it was getting closer and closer. The royal family got more and more frightened, and huddled toether in the castle.

The dragon enters.

The royal family all asked the creature what it was:

ROYAL FAMILY: Wh… wh… who are y… y… you?

NARRATOR: And the dragon replied:

DRAGON: I am the dragon of the enchanted forest. ROAR!

NARRATOR: Just when it looked like the royal family was going to become the dragon's dinner, they noticed that there was something stuck in the dragon's paw. It was a giant thorn! Now they knew that the dragon wasn't roaring in anger, it wasn't roaring in hunger, it was roaring in pain. The king grabbed hold of the giant thorn.

The King steps up to the dragon's paw.

And the queen held on to the king.

The queen holds on to the king.

The rest of the royal family made a line behind the king and the queen.

The rest of the royal family steps up behind the king and queen.

They pulled, and pulled, and PULLED!

The royals lean forward as the dragon leans backward. The royal family leans to the right as the dragon leans to the left. Continue moving to and fro.

And finally, with a last heave, they pulled the thorn from the dragon's paw. The dragon thanked the royal family.

DRAGON: Thank you!

The royal family respond to the dragon.

ROYAL FAMILY: You're welcome!

NARRATOR: And the dragon promised to protect the royal family always. In return the king decided to protect the dragon and the forest where he lived. And they all lived happily ever after!

Ask the students to take a bow and give and themselves a round of applause. If you have an audience, remind them to give the performers a round of applause. Rotate the children around to ensure they have a turn in each group, including the audience.

FINISH

Ask the children to lie down with their eyes closed.
Play the music you used to introduce the royal
family. Ask the children to imagine a castle and the
royal family who lives there. Ask them to imagine
the royal jewels found throughout the kingdom. As
they are resting with their eyes closed, sprinkle
some little sequins or stars around the room. Ask
them to open their eyes and find some 'royal
jewels'. They can draw a picture about this lesson
and decorate it with the jewels.

Extension

Continue to find opportunities in the story for the
characters to say a line. Build the story into a
performance by developing a simple script. You
might like to add the role of narrators.

Use simple instruments or music to enhance the
piece.

Divide the class into groups of 3–5. Ask them to
improvise a scene which includes a dragon and
members of the royal family.

Extracurricular Activities

- Create a simple castle by using a small cardboard
  box with cardboard tubes as the turrets.

- Children draw or paint their favourite character
  from the story.

- Write an adventure story set in the forest about
  a dragon or royal family.

- Sing the nursery rhyme 'Sing a Song of Sixpence'.

- Discuss the role of current royal families from
  around the world.

- Discuss how most coins from around the world
  picture a prominent royal or political figure.
  Collect and collate coins from different countries.

- Make crowns and tiaras.

- Discuss and discover dragons in mythology.
  Children can draw and cut out their own dragon.

- Create clay models of a dragon.
- Make a class dragon by decorating a cardboard box for the head. Attach a long length of fabric for the body to ensure the class can fit underneath.
- Create dragon shadow puppets.

TWO

DRAMATIC PLAY

Clowns and Comedy

This lesson has many activities. You may choose to do all of them, or select a few. You could spread these activities out over a number of classes.

Resources

- Comedy music.

WARM-UP
Silly Walks

Ask the children to find their own space in the room. Remind the children that they should not run or touch anybody else. Play the music during the activity as appropriate. When the students are settled, use the following instructions:

- *Let's all move around the space. Use your natural walk. But now we are going to try some silly walks.*

- *Can you make your bottom very big and stick it out while you walk? We are doing the big-bottom walk! Good work! Now let's go back to our natural walk.*

- *Can you push your tummy forward while you walk? Let's do the big-tummy walk! You really do look silly! Now let's come back to our natural walk.*

- *Can you stick your knees together? How can we walk with our knees stuck together? Good work, everyone. That was really hard, but it did look silly! Okay, back to your natural walk.*

- *Now let's try the bouncy-shoulders walk. Listen to the music and keep those shoulders bouncing. Good, now relax your shoulders.*

- *Let's try the knees-up-high walk. Bring them right up as high as you can as you move around. Wow, that was tricky! Good work.*

- *Let's try the wobbly walk. Can you make every part of your body wobble as you walk? Good! Now let's come back to our natural walk.*

- *Can you now try the chin-forward walk? Push it right out as you move around. Great work. You have some very silly ways of walking.*

- *What about the big-elbow walk? Wow! I like the way you are being careful of each other and not bumping together.*

- *Can you show me a different silly walk? Very good.*

- *Can you show me another silly walk?*

Silly Faces

Ask the children to stand in a circle.

- *We have seen how our bodies can look silly. Now let's try and make some silly faces, without using our hands or fingers.*

- *Let me see the different silly faces you can make.*

- *We're going to try and copy some of these faces. We will start here with me. Can you make this face?*

Pull a face that the children should copy.

- *Now it's your turn. We'll start with _____.*

Take it in turns so each child pulls a face that the rest of the group copy. Congratulate all of the children for trying the activity.

Presenting the Silly Walks, Silly Faces and a Silly Bow

Sit the children in the audience position. Select 2 or 3 children at a time to perform their silly walks and their silly faces. This should go for about 30–40 seconds. Play the comedy music and ask the children to present their silly walk and silly face. Repeat until all the children have presented.

Divide the class into two groups. One group will be the audience and the other the performers. Ask the performers to stand in a line offstage. Play the comedy music and ask the performers to walk into the performance space and parade around the stage twice. Once they have circled the stage twice, ask the children to stand in a line across the stage and take a 'silly bow'. Remind the audience group to give a round of applause after the performance. Ask the children to exit the space. Swap the groups over and repeat.

You may choose to end the lesson here, or continue with the following activities.

FOCUS
Fake Trips

Ask the children to sit in the audience position.

Demonstrate a 'fake trip'. Walk from one side of the space towards the other side. When you get to the centre of the space, pretend to trip over by tucking one foot behind the other while you continue to move forward. Stumble forward before standing upright again, as if you are regaining your balance. Continue walking to the other side of the space.

Before starting the activity, explain to the children the importance of safety. The children will most likely want to fall over, so you will need to determine how many of the children will have a turn at once, and if there is enough space for falling or tripping.

Select some children to line up along one side of the space and instruct them to demonstrate the fake fall or trip. Continue until all the children have had a turn.

Once the children have had a few turns at tripping over, ask them to sit in the audience position. Select one or two children to enter the performance space and present their fake trip. Explain that the falls are funnier for the audience if they look spontaneous and real. The children who are performing may like to add a sound or a line, for example: 'I'm just on my way to the shops... whoa!' or 'Is that a banana peel on the ground?'

Remind the audience to give a round of applause after the performance.

The Big Crash

In this activity, the children crash into each other and fall backwards. To do the fall, start with your knees bent. Reach your hands behind you to assist lowering your body on to the floor, landing with your bottom first then rolling onto your back. A backward fall can finish with your legs in the air for added comic effect.

Divide the class into pairs and ask the children to sit in the audience position. Select one pair and ask them to stand on opposite sides of the performance space. Ask the pair to complete the following:

- Both children walk towards the centre of the room.

- As they reach each other, they bring both hands in front of their bodies.

- As they touch each other's hands, they push off each other's hands and fall backwards.

Ensure the children practise this in slow motion first.

Repeat until all the pairs of children have performed. Extend the activity by performing with the music and adding a silly walk and a silly face. Build the exercise by asking them to think of a line for their character before they walk. For example: younger children might do something like the following:

> PERSON A: I'm going this way!
>
> PERSON A *walks across the room.*
>
> PERSON B: I'm going this way!
>
> PERSON B *walks from the other direction. They 'crash' in the centre.*

For older children, encourage them to think about where their character is going and why. For example:

> PERSON A: Oh no! I'm going to be late for the party!
>
> PERSON A *walks towards the centre of the room.*
>
> PERSON B: Oh dear! I'm running late for work!
>
> PERSON B *walks from the other side. They 'crash' in the centre.*

As the children become more confident with performing and speaking in front of an audience, encourage them to build the performance further. For example:

> PERSON A: Help! Won't somebody help me!
>
> PERSON A *walks across the room.*
>
> PERSON B (*as the hero*): I hear someone calling for help! Don't worry, I'll save you!
>
> PERSON B *walks from the other side. They 'crash' in the centre.*

Ask the children to exit the space. Swap the groups over and repeat. Remind the children to give a round of applause after the performance.

Handshake

Divide the class into pairs and ask everyone to sit in the audience position. Select one pair to enter the performance space, standing on opposite sides from each other. Ask the pair to complete the following:

- Person A waves hello to Person B.
- Person B waves hello to Person A.
- Both walk towards the centre of the space with right hand outstretched as if to shake hands.
- As they meet in the centre, the backs of their hands brush past each other and they continue to walk to the opposite side of the room.
- Both stop and turn back to each other.
- Both have a confused look on their faces.
- Both look at their own hands, then scratch their heads in confusion.
- Both shrug and walk towards each other again with their hands outstretched.
- They continue passing each other, missing the handshake, until eventually they connect.
- They perform an exaggerated handshake.

Ask the children to exit the space. Invite more pairs to enter the space. Repeat until all pairs have had a turn. Remind the children to give a round of applause after each performance.

Statues

Divide the class into pairs and ask the children to sit in the audience position. Begin by selecting one pair and ask Person A to stand in the performance space. Ask Person B to enter the performance space and for the pair to complete the following:

- Person A imagines they are a statue in the garden or a gallery.
- Person B enters the garden and observes the statue then turns to face the audience.
- Person A changes position.
- Person B looks at the statue again, scratches head, and turns to face the audience again. Encourage big facial expressions.
- Person A changes position again.
- Continue until Person A has made 3–5 statues.
- Swap the children so Person B becomes the statue and Person A the observer.

Do this a few times with different pairs. Next, invite all the children to stand and find a space to work with their partner. You may choose to freeze the whole class and ask them to watch a particular pair at work during this time. Extend this activity by adding some of the following elements:

- The observer begins to mime eating their lunch, puts it down to receive a phone call (or another distraction). The statue comes to life and begins to eat the lunch.
- The statue pulls silly faces behind the observer's back.
- As the observer moves around, the statue comes to life and begins to follow them around the space.
- The statue steals something from the back pocket of the observer.

Performing Clowns

Divide the class into pairs and ask them to present one, or a combination, of the skits explored during the lesson. You may like to play the music as the children are rehearsing and when they present their work.

FINISH

Laugh Lines

Select one child to sit on a seat. The rest of the children form a line in front of the chair. The children must try to make the seated person smile or laugh without touching them. They can try silly faces, walks, noises or lines. If the child on the seat laughs, they must change places with the child who made them laugh. Continue until most children have had a turn on the seat.

Extension

Divide the class into pairs or small groups. Using the activities from this lesson, extend them into an improvisation and give them a setting. For example: they may be:

- o in a restaurant
- o at the museum
- o purchasing something
- o in the classroom
- o at work
- o napping

Extracurricular Activities

- Have a silly-face competition.
- Have a circus-skills visit/excursion or performance.
- Discuss what makes us laugh.
- Make a collection of silly stories.
- Make a clown nose by painting an egg-carton cup red and attaching elastic.
- Draw a silly face. Experiment with different sizes, shapes and colours.
- Bring joke books to class and encourage the children to tell a joke in front of the class.
- For older children, introduce *Commedia dell'Arte*, the Italian masked comedy.

Groups and Shapes

Resources

- Three different instruments (for example: a tambourine, a triangle and a drum).

WARM-UP
Levels

Ask the children to find their own space in the room. Remind the children that they should not run or touch anybody else. When the students are settled, use the following instructions:

- *Can you walk around the space? Good.*

- *I am going to make a sound with the triangle. When you hear the triangle you are going to find a 'high' way of walking. Great work.*

- *Now when I play a beat on the drum, can you find a 'low' way of moving? Good work.*

- *Let's try the triangle again. Good, you remembered, we walk high for the triangle.*

- *Now how do you walk when I play the drum? Excellent.*

- *Now I'm going to add another one. When you hear the sound of the tambourine, can you find a 'medium' way of moving? Fantastic.*

- *I am going to test you now and see if you remember all of them.*

Continue to switch between the three different sounds. Encourage the children to find different ways to move as they are low, medium and high, for example: slowly, quickly, quietly, loudly, as if walking through thick mud, as if walking on snow, as if walking up sand dunes. When the children are comfortable moving in the different levels, extend the activity by using the following instructions:

- *Walking low, medium and high is called walking at different levels. Now I'm going to ask you to freeze in each level. Are you ready?*

- *Let's move around to the drum.*

- *Make sure you don't crawl or slide around. Can you find a way of moving low on two feet? Good. Ready? Freeze!*

Repeat the activity several times with a frozen position at each level.

Shapes

Ask the children to find their own space in the room. Remind the children that they should not touch anybody else. As the children engage in the following activity, show some of the work. Compliment the use of levels, good freezes and imaginative ideas.

- *Now I'm going to see how you can change your body to make different shapes.*

- *I'm going to give you a shape, then count backwards from five to one. When I reach the number one, I would like you to freeze in that shape.*

- *You'll have to think and move very quickly.*

- *Can you be:*
   o *a tall building?*
   o *a small flower?*
   o *a tree with wide branches?*
   o *a pointy star?*
   o *a round ball?*
   o *a flat pancake?*

- *Finally, stand naturally.*

Divide the class into groups of 2 (if there are odd numbers create one group of 3).

- *Let's make some more shapes. This time I will count backwards from ten to one. You will still have to work very quickly together.*

- *Can you work together with your partner to be:*
   o *a bucket and spade?*
   o *a drink with a straw?*
   o *a pair of Wellingtons?*
   o *a cup and plate?*
   o *a tree in a pot?*
   o *a chicken with an egg?*
   o *a toothbrush?*
   o *a throne?*

- *Finally, stand naturally.*

Divide the class in groups of 3.

- *Let's make some more shapes. I will count backwards from ten to one again. You will still have to work very quickly together.*

- *Can you work together with your group to be:*
  - o *a dinosaur?*
  - o *a teapot?*
  - o *a butterfly?*
  - o *a bird?*
  - o *an elephant?*
  - o *a hamburger?*
- *Finally, stand naturally.*

Divide the class into groups of five or six.

- *Let's make some more shapes in our new groups. I will count backwards from ten to one. You will still have to work very quickly together.*

- *Can you be:*
  - o *an enchanted tree?*
  - o *a bridge?*
  - o *a house with a door and a chimney?*
  - o *a rainbow?*
  - o *a fish in a fishbowl?*
- *Finally, stand naturally.*

The whole group can attempt the following shapes. Give them a slow countdown from ten to one. Observe the leaders and the followers. Remind the children to look around and see how the shape is emerging so they can add to the shape as it evolves. Also point out that they may need to change their original idea to fit into the shape as it evolves. Encourage and compliment teamwork, good listening skills, adapting to new ideas, sharing ideas verbally, leadership and participation.

- *Let's make some more shapes as a whole group. I will still count backwards from ten to one. Can you all work together?*

- *Don't forget to use different levels. Can you be:*
  - o *a cake with candles?*
  - o *a bowl of noodles?*
  - o *a forest?*
  - o *a castle with a moat?*
  - o *a snake/dragon/caterpillar?*
  - o *an octopus?*
- *Finally, stand naturally.*

FOCUS
Guess the Shape

Sit the children in the audience position. Select 1, 2 or 3 children to enter the performance space. Whisper a shape, object or place to the children. For example: ask the children to create the shape of a star, an octopus, or a frozen picture (tableau) of 'at the restaurant'. The performers must try to get into the suggested position and the audience tries to guess what they are doing. You can also select an object from the room that the children have to imitate with their bodies. You may want to finish the class here, or continue with the following activities.

Symmetry

Sit the children in the audience position. Select one child to enter the performance space. Ask the child to hold both arms and legs out wide. Highlight the line of symmetry by 'drawing' an imaginary line down the centre of the child. Explain that a symmetrical shape has to be the same on both sides of the central line.

Select two more children and stand them either side of the first child. Ask the two new children to put the hand closest to the central child on their shoulder. Ask the new children to place the other hand on their hip. Again, 'draw' an imaginary line of symmetry and discuss with the class.

Ask one of the outside children to put both hands on their hips. Discuss this with the class, asking questions such as:

• *Is this symmetrical?*

• *Why not?*

Continue creating symmetrical shapes with other children and continue to check for understanding. Build on the activity so you make a symmetrical shape with everyone. Begin with one child. Continue to add to the shape until the whole class is involved. Take a photo of the whole-class shape and discuss the lines of symmetry.

Asymmetry

Depending on the age and ability of your class, this also may be a good opportunity to discuss asymmetry. Again, begin with just one child. Ask the child to create a symmetrical shape then to change the shape so that it is asymmetrical. Discuss asymmetry with the class, how asymmetrical shapes must be different on both sides. Continue to explore more asymmetrical shapes with more children.

Picture Postcard

Ask the children to sit in the audience position. Inform the children that they will be creating postcards of different places. Nominate a place, and select one child to enter the performance space and hold a position which suggests something or someone from the nominated place. Ensure that all children are facing the audience. Continue building the picture by selecting the children to add on to the picture, one by one.

For example: the beach:

- Child 1 enters and freezes in sandcastle-making position.
- Child 2 enters and freezes in swimming position.
- Child 3 enters and freezes in seagull position.
- Child 4 enters and copies seagull position.
- Child 5 enters and freezes in umbrella position over Child 1.

Continue until all the children are a part of the postcard. Stand in front of the postcard image and either mime taking a photo, or take a real photo so the children can observe their work. You may also wish to divide the class into two groups. Group 1 is the audience and Group 2 is the postcard. Ensure all performers face their audience. Encourage the children to use a variety of levels.

Other ideas for a postcard include:

- o a haunted house
- o a jungle

- o a beach
- o a restaurant
- o a zoo
- o under the sea.

Extension: Postcard Coming to Life

Place the whole class in one of the postcards from the previous activity. Explain that when you clap your hands, the postcard will 'come to life'. Discuss with the children how their part of the postcard may come to life, for example: the umbrella might only sway in the breeze, while the seagulls might fly around the room. Encourage dialogue and improvisation. After a few moments, call 'freeze'. Break the class up into smaller groups and repeat the activity.

Extracurricular Activities

- Explore and identify different shapes including levels, symmetry and asymmetry.

- Make a shape mural.

- Find symmetry in classical and contemporary architecture. For example: Tower Bridge, the Taj Mahal, the Eiffel Tower.

- Try some simple math exercises – adding groups of ones, twos, threes, etc.

- Read popular children's books and ask the children to imitate an object, shape or place from the book.

- Make playdough shapes.

- Make cookies or biscuits and cut out with different shapes.

- Go on an excursion to a local gallery or art museum to explore and identify shape in art.

- Discuss the importance of teamwork, good listening, leadership skills and sharing ideas.

Instruments, Music and Sound

Resources

- Three large pieces of fabric in different colours (optional).
- A collection of instruments.

WARM-UP
Follow the Action

Ask the children to sit in a circle. When the children are ready, use the following instructions:

- *I am going to see if you can copy me, are you ready?*

Begin by clapping a beat with your hands.

- *Well done. Now I'm going to change the action. Ready?*

Clap a beat on your legs.

- *Well done. Now I am going to keep changing it, and you will have to be ready to change the action with me.*

Continue the activity changing the action so that you are: tapping on your knees, shoulders, head, the floor, crossing your arms and tapping on your elbows and so on. End the sequence by clapping your hands again.

- *Well done. Now it's your turn.*
- *We will now go around the circle and when it's your turn, you can do any movement you like, or you can copy some of the ones we just did.*
- *We are going to try and copy every move until we get all the way around the circle.*
- *Let's go. Starting with _____ .*

Continue until all the children have directed a movement.

Storm Soundscape

Ask the children to remain seated in a circle. When the children are ready, use the following instructions:

- *We are now going to copy my movement.*
- *It's very important that we don't talk during this, as I want you to listen really carefully.*
- *When we finish, I am going to ask you what this reminded you of.*
- *Let's begin:*

- o *Rubbing hands together (wind)*
- o *Fast little claps (pitter-patter rain)*
- o *Louder claps (rain)*
- o *Clapping on laps (heavy rain)*
- o *Clapping on the floor (rain and hail)*
- o *Stomping on the floor (thunder)*
- o *Clapping on the floor (rain and hail)*
- o *Clapping on laps (heavy rain)*
- o *Louder claps (rain)*
- o *Fast little claps (pitter-patter rain)*
- o *Rubbing hands together (wind)*

- *Good work, now can you please tell me what you thought those sounds reminded you of?* (Hopefully the children will guess a rainstorm passing over.)

- *Well done, shall we do it again? This time, listen very carefully and think of a storm passing as we make these sounds.*

Repeat the activity.

Discuss

- *We have clapped and made tapping sounds with our bodies and we have made a rainstorm with our bodies. What other sounds can we make with our body? What parts of our body can we use to make sound?*

Sounds

After completing the discussion, ask the children to remain seated in a circle. When the children are ready, use the following instructions:

- *Now let's try and make some new sounds.*

- *I will start. Can you try and copy my sounds?*

Create some random and varied sounds with your voice and ask the children to repeat them back to you. For example: a bird chirping, the sound of the wind in the trees, a horse galloping, etc.

- *Now it's your turn.*

- *Who would like to make a new sound?*
- *Good, let's all try and copy _____.*
- *Who's next?*

Either select a few children or ask each child to make a sound for the rest of the class to copy.

Ocean Sounds

Ask the children to stand in a circle. When the children are ready, use the following instructions:

- *We are going to make some sounds from the beach.*
- *Who can make some sounds, using their body or voice to make the sounds of the waves? Good. Let's do it all together.*
- *Can you make the sound of the waves? Let's move our arms as well to make the shape of the waves getting bigger. Good work.*
- *What other sounds do we hear at the beach?*
- *What about seagulls? What do they sound like? Good, let's move our arms out wide like wings.*
- *What about the wind? What sounds can we make for the wind? How can we move our bodies to be like the wind?*

Continue making sounds that will be familiar to the children. Ask for their suggestions of sounds they would hear at the beach.

FOCUS
Ocean Soundscape

Divide the class into three groups: seagulls, wind and waves. Nominate three different areas of the room for each group. You may wish to use a large piece of fabric to help define each space. When the children are ready, use the following instructions:

- *I am now going to be a musical conductor.*

- *Do you know what a conductor does? That's right, they are at the front of the orchestra telling the musicians when to play, how loud they must play and how fast to play.*

- *When I raise my arm like this, you are going to get loud.*

- *When I lower my arm like this, you will be softer.*

- *When I make a fist like this, you will be totally quiet.*

- *Let's try and make the ocean orchestra.*

Orchestrate a simple soundscape based on the ocean. Bring one group in at time, then two together, then all three. Experiment with different levels of volume. Finish in silence.

Jungle Sounds

Sit the children in a circle. When the children are ready, use the following instructions:

- *Let's now create a different orchestra.*

- *This time, it's called the jungle orchestra.*

- *What sort of sounds do you think we might hear in the jungle?*

Suggestions include, insects, birds, monkeys, low growls and hissing snakes.

Divide the class into three groups and allocate each group a different animal/insect. (Note: if you are teaching younger children, it may be best to keep them in a single group.) Nominate three different areas of the room for each group. You may wish to use a large piece of fabric to help define each space.

When the children are ready, use the following instructions:

- *Let's begin.*
- *Make sure you follow my instructions as the conductor.*

Start by introducing each group one at a time. Remind the children to use the sounds they mentioned at the start of the activity. Introduce the sounds and keep them going until you build a whole class soundscape. Slowly reduce the sounds until you have silence.

If you are short of time, you may choose to end the class here, or continue with the following activities.

Instruments

Demonstrate the different sounds each of the instruments you have chosen can make. Ask one of the children to choose which instrument they think would be best to use to create a sound for the beach. Ask different children the best instrument for some of the following:

- o a jungle
- o a spooky house
- o a marching band
- o a fairy land
- o under the sea
- o a monster
- o a princess
- o someone in a hurry
- o an aeroplane
- o thunder
- o lightning
- o a snake
- o a bird
- o footsteps
- o flying

A Soundscape Story

Narrate a simple story and ask the children to create the sounds with body percussion, their voices and the instruments. You can either get the whole class to make each of the sounds, or nominate which sounds particular children will make.

The following is an example of an adventure in the jungle.

- *Once there was a brave explorer who decided to go to the jungle. He walked and he walked and he walked all through the jungle. He could hear the birds high in the trees. And then he heard the leaves rustling. He looked up and saw the monkeys. He took a photo with his camera. He came to some squelchy mud, and had to walk through it with his big boots. Then everything was quiet.*

- *He looked around and could hear some insects. They were getting closer and closer. Suddenly the insects were all around him. They started biting his arms. He screamed out. And then suddenly the insects were gone. And everything was quiet again.*

- *Then the wind came rustling through the trees. The sky got darker and then it started to pitter-patter with rain. The rain got heavier and then there was a loud thunderclap. There was lightning and the explorer started to run.*

- *He ran and he ran and he ran. Finally, the thunder and lightning and hard rain stopped. There was just a soft sound of the last drops of rain.*

- *The explorer could hear waves far away in the distance. He walked quickly down the hill. He could hear seagulls in the distance. Then the waves were getting louder and louder. He had reached the beach.*

- *He looked out saw a big ship. The ship had a long, low horn. The explorer called out for help! He waved his arms and splashed into the water. He was saved!*

Either finish the story here or ask the children to add to it, finding new opportunities for sounds. You may also sit the children in a circle and, one at a time, ask them to add one line to the story. You could record this story and make illustrations to create a movie with your class (using movie-making software).

FINISH
Guess the Sound

Sit the children in a circle and select one child to enter the middle of the circle, with their eyes closed. Create a simple and recognisable sound and ask the child in the centre to try and identify the sound. Once they have guessed correctly, choose another child. Ideas include:

o rattling keys
o opening or closing a door
o tearing a piece of paper in half
o scrunching up paper
o cutting a piece of paper with scissors
o yawning
o scratching your nails on a hard surface
o whistling

Increase the difficulty of the sounds as the children become more confident with the activity. You can also select more than one child to guess the sound, or divide the class into teams and keep score of correct guesses.

Extension

Divide the class into small groups and ask them to create a soundscape using voice, body percussion and instruments. Ask the audience to close their eyes or turn away from the performers and try to guess the soundscape. Ideas include:

o a haunted house
o a playground
o another planet
o a machine
o the zoo
o an African safari
o the city
o a library

Extracurricular Activities

- Discuss different musical instruments, orchestras, bands and unique instruments from around the world.
- Make instruments from recycled materials and make a band.
- Invite a band or musician to come and perform.
- Discuss different styles and genres of music. Ask the children to bring a copy of their favourite song.
- Discuss the role of music around the world.
- Discuss how the world would be different if there was no music.
- Write a story about a magical instrument.
- Draw or paint a picture of an instrument or band.
- Invite the children to bring in an instrument from home and encourage them to play it in front of the class.
- Watch a clip from a popular children's film and discuss its soundtrack and sound effects.
- Create simple movies using movie-making software and emphasise sound effects.

Mime

Mime conveys dramatic meaning through action and gesture. It communicates narrative and can enhance the meaning of the subtext. For young children, mime is a wonderful tool: it is non-threatening, accessible, quick and requires little previous knowledge or skill. It is also a perfect medium for children from non-English speaking backgrounds.

Resources

- Music.

WARM-UP
Body Awareness

Sit the children in a circle. When the children are ready, use the following instructions:

- *We are going to warm up our whole bodies. First let's look at all the different parts.*

- *Can you look at:*
    - *your fingers?*
    - *your hands?*
    - *your arms?*
    - *your shoulders?*
    - *your chest?*
    - *your tummy?*
    - *the top of your legs?*
    - *your ankles?*
    - *your feet?*
    - *your toes?*

- *Now let's wake up each of these body parts.*

- *Can you please stand up and find a space?*

Play the music. During this exploration of body parts, insist that there is no touching one another and no talking. Encourage the children to use large, slow movements. Incorporate some stretching and balancing exercises into the warm-up.

- *When I call out a part of the body, can you find a way to make it move to the music?*

Mirrors

Stand in front of the class and ask the children to stand in the space. When the children are ready, use the following instructions:

- *You are going to become my mirror.*

- *When I move, you are going to try and do exactly what I do at the same time, just like when we are standing in front of a real mirror.*

- *Ready? Let's start.*

Raise first one arm up and down, then the other, then both arms together.

• *Very good. Now let's try some harder movements.*

Explore more movements, gestures and facial expressions. Explore different body parts. You might consider playing some gentle music as you work to engage the children and bring focus to the activity.

Mirrors in Pairs

Divide the class into pairs. One of the children is Person A and the other child is Person B. Ask the children to face each other as if they are looking in a mirror. Person A will lead the movement for a few minutes, while Person B follows their movements. Swap the children, so Person B leads the movement and Person A follows. Continue alternating the leader and the mirror.

Sit the children in the audience position. Ask some of the children to take it in turns to show their work. Compliment good focus and concentration. Compliment good teamwork and observation skills. Remind the children to applaud the performers after they complete their presentation.

Discuss

Ask the students what you need to remember when we are miming. Explain that you are going to mime 'peeling a banana'. Execute the mime very badly – fast, sloppy movements, no focus. Ask if it looked like peeling a banana. The children will say no! Ask the class how you would make it better. The point of this discussion is to establish some basic rules of mime; the action must be slow and controlled with large, clear movements and the performer must imagine the action to be real. Ask the students again what you need to remember when they are miming. Lead the students to discuss that the most important thing when you are miming is using your imagination.

FOCUS
Emotions and Mime

Sit the children in a circle. When the children are ready, use the following instructions:

- *We are now going to work some more in mime.*
- *Have you heard that word before? In drama, it means that we do action without sound.*
- *I am going to show you an emotion (or feeling). I'm not going to use any sound.*
- *I'm going to do the emotion in mime. When I use mime, I have to turn off my voice. This means I can only use my face and my body.*
- *Let's see if you can guess which emotion I'm doing.*

Turn away from the class as though you're angry. You might also put your hands on your hips, shake your fist, cross your arms or raise your shoulders.

- *Can you guess?*
- *That's right! I was pretending to be angry.*
- *How did you know?*

Children may say things such as your hands were on your hips, you had an angry face, you were shaking your finger at the class or that your shoulders were forward.

- *Good, now it's your turn.*
- *Let's all show anger in mime.*

Give the children a few moments to mime anger. Compliment good facial expressions and gestures.

- *Now I'm going to choose somebody to show a different emotion.*
- *Let's see if we can guess what this next one is.*

Select a student or a few students at a time to show the rest of the class a different emotion. Whisper suggestions and then ask the rest of the class to guess:

- o scared
- o surprised
- o happy
- o sad
- o sleepy
- o confused

Simple Mimes

Ask the children to find their own space in the room. When the students are settled, use the following instructions:

- *We are going to practise some simple, everyday mimes by ourselves.*

- *Remember to turn off your voice and only use your face and body when you mime.*

- *Can you mime each of these actions as I call them out?*

  o *eat with a spoon*
  o *brush your hair*
  o *put on your shoes*
  o *wash your face*
  o *read a book*

Mime Exercise

Ask the children to find a space of their own and mime the following actions. Encourage the children to use large, slow, focused movements as they mime:

  o bouncing a ball
  o brushing their teeth
  o riding a bike
  o picking a flower
  o talking on the phone
  o drinking a hot drink
  o blowing up a balloon
  o sweeping the floor
  o painting a picture
  o taking a photo
  o carrying a heavy object
  o washing their hands

You may like to extend this activity with a range of different actions from the child's own experience.

Pass the Mime

Ask the children to sit in a circle and use the following instructions:

- *We are going to pass around an imaginary object.*
- *Remember, this is mime, so we have to turn off our voices and make our facial expressions and our bodies very interesting.*
- *I will start, then I'm going to pass it to _____.*
- *They will pass it to _____ and they will pass it on and so on.*
- *Are you ready? Here it is.*

Mime picking up a very heavy object. Pass it to the first child in the circle. Encourage the whole class to remain focused on the object as it moves around the circle.

- *Good work! Now I'm going to ask you what you imagined you were passing.*
- *_____, what did you pretend it was?*

Continue asking a few children. They will all want to share their ideas, so to save time and maintain momentum, ask them to turn to the person next to them and tell them what they imagined the heavy object was.

Repeat the exercise, but this time go the other way around the circle.

- *Okay, now we are going to pass something very different. Are you ready?*

Mime passing something tiny or precious. Again, select some children to tell you what they imagined it was.

- *Now this is the last one.*
- *I'm really sorry to have to do this to you.*
- *Are you ready?*

Mime picking up something really smelly. You might imagine an old, dirty, smelly sock. Pick it up off the floor with two fingers and hold your nose with the other hand. Pass it to the first child in the circle. Continue as above. When it gets back to you, mime throwing it away. Again, discuss with the children what they thought it was.

You may choose to end the class here, or to
continue with the following activity.

Miming a Story

Narrate a simple story for the children to act out in
mime. For example: your story could be about the
children's day. Begin with sleeping, yawning,
stretching, eating breakfast and brushing your teeth,
then walking to school, holding an umbrella in the
rain, jumping over puddles, finding a beautiful
flower and arriving at school. This could be done as
whole class, or you could sit the children in
audience position and select a few children to
perform at a time. Encourage the audience to give a
round of applause as the performers take a bow.
Try a range of different simple stories. Ideas include:

  o a picnic at the park
  o a visit to the zoo
  o choosing some new shoes at the shoe shop
  o making a giant sandwich or a big cake

FINISH
Guess the Mime

Sit the children in audience position. Select one child to stand in front of the audience. Either whisper a mime to the child or ask them to think of an everyday action to mime to the audience. The audience must try to guess the mime.

Extension

Divide the class into groups of 3–5. Ask them to tell a story in mime. They can either select one person to be the narrator as the others mime the story, or you could give them one of the following scenarios to improvise. You could also consider selecting a piece of music and asking the groups to create a mime to match the music.

- o a robbery in a gallery
- o a fussy customer changing their mind in a restaurant
- o a person who gets lost in the jungle
- o a birthday party when the child doesn't like the presents

When all the groups have had 5–10 minutes to prepare, sit the children in the audience position and show each group's work. Compliment good focus and concentration, good teamwork and miming skills. Remind the children to applaud the performers after each performance.

Extracurricular Activities

- Use photos or magazine and newspaper pictures to identify different emotions. Make an 'emotion chart' by sorting the pictures into groups.

- Read simple children's stories and encourage the children to act out parts in mime.

- Bring some mirrors into your room and encourage the children to observe their own face and how it changes with different emotions. Encourage 'silly faces'.

- Draw a large face and ask the children to draw the features in a particular emotion.
- Link the body-awareness activity to making handprints, fingerprints and footprints.
- Make whole-body pictures by tracing around each student on a large piece of paper. Decorate and arrange by height. Repeat the activity outdoors using chalk to trace.
- Discuss disabilities; explain that some people cannot talk, hear, see, walk, etc. Discuss how life would be different without communicating vocally.
- Try 10–30 minutes of silence, using mime for all communication.

Object Transformation

Object transformation is where an object's main
purpose is transformed into another purpose, and
then another and another. A simple example of this
is to turn a bedsheet into a cape, then waves on the
ocean. Object transformation taps into a child's
sense of play as well as their imagination, especially
in early childhood.

Resources

- A newspaper.
- Upbeat music.
- A long tube or stick, and another
  object such as a bucket.
- A collection of 5–10 miscellaneous
  objects.
- A piece of fabric to cover the
  miscellaneous objects.

WARM-UP
Something with Something

Ask the children to find their own space in the room. Remind the children that they should not run or touch anybody else. When the students are settled, use the following instructions:

- *Let's all walk around the space. When I call 'freeze', you are going to be as still as a statue. Ready? Freeze. Excellent work.*

- *Let's move around the space again. This time when I call 'freeze', I am going to ask you to touch something with a body part that I call out. Ready? Freeze.*

- *Can you touch something black with your finger? Good!*

- *Back to your natural walk. Freeze!*

- *Can you touch something soft with your head? Good work. I like the way you're listening and being careful of each other.*

Try a whole range of textures, colours and surfaces. For instance, touch:

- o something shiny with your arm
- o something blue with your foot
- o a wall with your back
- o something tall with your ear

Musical Islands

Ask the children sit to one side of the performance space. Spread the newspaper sheets around the space and explain to the children to imagine that these pieces of newspaper have been transformed into islands. Play some upbeat music and ask the children to move around the room without touching the islands with their feet.

When the music stops, the children must quickly move and stand on an island. If the newspaper rips, the children must find a different island.

Remove any piece of newspaper with a rip or tear, or if it becomes too scrunched up.

Continue until only three islands remain.

Newspaper Transformation

Ask the children to sit in a circle. When the students are settled, hold up a newspaper to the children and use the following instructions:

- *Who can tell me what this is?*
- *That's right, it's a newspaper. But we are going to turn this newspaper into all kinds of different things today.*
- *We are going to transform the newspaper.*
- *First, we are going to warm up the newspaper, just like we need to warm up our bodies for drama.*

Give each child a sheet of newspaper.

- *Can you make your newspaper go very high?*
- *Can you make your newspaper move very low?*
- *Can you make your newspaper look very stiff and strong?*
- *How can you make your newspaper look floppy?*
- *Can you make it very flat?*
- *Great work, everyone, I think our newspaper is ready for some more tricks.*
- *Now see if you can you turn your piece of newspaper into a:*
  - *hat*
  - *bed*
  - *shoe*
  - *bag*
  - *cape*
  - *ball*
- *Well done, everyone.*
- *You all did a wonderful job transforming your newspaper.*

Collect and discard the newspaper.

Discuss

Ask the children to return to the circle.
Discuss how we can make something into
something else by using our body, face, sound
and imagination. Your conversation might go
something like:

- *When you turned your newspaper into a cape,*
  it wasn't really a cape, but I could tell it was
  because some of you looked like a superhero.
  You changed your face to look very brave and
  important, you reached one arm forward to
  look like you were flying. But there was
  something else working that is really
  important. Can you guess what it is? What do
  need when we are pretending? That's right,
  our imaginations.

FOCUS
Object Transformation

Remain sitting in a circle. Place a long thin object in the centre of the circle. This could be a long cardboard tube, a child-size broom handle, a metre ruler or a rhythm stick. When the students are settled, use the following instructions:

- *We are going to be using our imaginations a lot more in this next activity. You are all going to have a turn, but we will be coming in one at a time. First, it's my turn.*

- *I am going to pick up this stick and turn it into something else. I want you to try and guess what it is. Are you ready? Okay, here's the first one.*

Mime using the stick as a hairbrush. The children should immediately guess the mime. Try another one. It is important that you keep the actions within the children's understanding. Try actions from everyday activities. Ask the children to guess the mime.

- *Great work. Now it's your turn. I'm going to ask you to come into the circle and pick up the stick.*

Ask the children to enter the space, one at a time, and use the stick as something else. Most children will have an idea of their own, or repeat one that has been performed already. Some may use sound, words or simple gesture and mime. Applaud each child as they complete the activity. It is important that you don't force the children to participate. If any children are reluctant to have a turn, give them time to think about it and offer the option of getting back to them. You may also ask them to enter the circle with a friend and present a mime together. You could also whisper an idea to them or enter the circle with them. If the child is still reluctant, do not force them. They are still learning by watching the other children.

You may need to suggest some of the following ideas:

- o a toothbrush
- o a walking stick
- o a tightrope

- o a stirring spoon
- o an eating spoon
- o the steering wheel of a car
- o a microphone
- o a pen or pencil
- o a telephone
- o handlebars
- o an ice cream
- o a rolling pin
- o a telescope
- o a corn on the cob

Repeat the activity with a different object.
Remember to demonstrate some ideas before the
children have a turn. You may wish to use a bucket
or a large container. Ideas could include:

- o a steering wheel
- o a bowl
- o a drum
- o a shoe
- o a hat
- o an earring
- o a toilet
- o a pillow
- o a helmet
- o a seat
- o a computer
- o a birthday cake

You can extend this activity further by placing two
or three objects in the centre. Use different things
such as a scarf, a rope, a plastic cone, an old teapot
or a hoop. As the children become more
comfortable with the exercise, their confidence and
ideas will begin to grow.

FINISH
What's Missing?

Place a number of small objects in the centre – for example: a feather, a small toy, a pencil, a shoe and some keys. Ask the children to observe and memorise the objects. Place a sheet of fabric over the objects. There are different ways you can continue.

Select one child to close his or her eyes while you remove one of the objects. Ask the child to open their eyes, remove the fabric and ask them to identify 'what's missing'. Continue to add more objects.

Ask all the children to close their eyes. Remove one of the objects. Ask all the children to open their eyes. Select one child at a time to guess which object is missing.

For older children, remove more than one object at a time. Or continue to add objects until there are ten or more to memorise.

Extension

Divide the class into pairs or groups of 3–5 and ask them to present a scene in a restaurant or at the shops. Give each pair one object and ask them to transform it at least three different times. Sit the class in the audience position and show each of the groups' work. Ensure the audience gives the performers a round of applause after each scene.

Extracurricular Activities

• Visit a recycling centre. Discuss how objects can be turned from one thing to another.

• Make an odds-and-ends collage.

• Examine the objects in your class and categorise the different materials such as plastic, metal, wood or fabric.

• Create a chart and explore simple math tasks, such as simple bar graphs or counting activities.

- Make an orchestra or band with a variety of objects and recycled materials.
- Explore magnets and magnetic objects.
- Bring in a mystery object and ask the children to guess what it might be used for.
- Explore sorting and counting activities.
- See how many uses your class can come up with for an empty tin. For example: it could be for storing scissors or pens, to make a pair of stilts, a tealight holder, a miniature golf course or a pot plant. Repeat the same exercise with an egg carton or a cardboard box.

Making Puppets

Using puppets is a wonderful way to engage all students, especially those who are particularly self-conscious or from a non-English speaking background.

Resources

- 'Where is Thumbkin?'
- 'Two Little Dickie Birds'.
- A newspaper.
- A few songs such as 'Twinkle Twinkle Little Star' or 'ABC'.

WARM-UP
Nursery Rhyme Finger Puppets

Ask the children to sit in a circle. Use your fingers to mime the actions of the songs below. When the students are settled, use the following instructions:

- Sing the song 'Where is Thumbkin?' (to the tune of 'Frère Jacques'):

  Where is Thumbkin? Where is Thumbkin?
  Here I am! Here I am!
  How are you today, sir?
  Very well, I thank you.
  Run away. Run away.

- Sing the song 'Two Little Dickie Birds':

  Two little dickie birds, sitting on a wall,
  One named Peter,
  One named Paul.
  'Fly away, Peter!
  Fly away, Paul!'
  'Come back, Peter!
  Come back, Paul!'

Repeat 'Two Little Dickie Birds' using the names of students in your class instead of 'Peter' and 'Paul'.

Hand Puppets

Remain sitting in a circle. Ask the children to pretend that one of their hands is a talking puppet. The fingers become the top jaw and the thumb becomes the bottom jaw. The 'puppet' talks by opening and closing the hand. Repeat the song 'Two Little Dickie Birds' using the hand puppets. Encourage the children open and close the mouth to speak the words 'Hello, Peter!' and 'Hello, Paul!'

Puppet Emotion

Remain sitting in a circle. Ask the children to just use one of their hand puppets to explore the following emotions.

- *Can you make your puppet look:*
  - *happy?* (hand 'bounces')
  - *sad?* (hand droops forward)
  - *excited?* (hand moves fast)
  - *shy?* (hand moves towards or behind the body)
  - *scared?* (hand shakes, mouth opens to scream)
  - *angry?* (hand is tense, small shakes)
  - *sleepy?* (hand 'yawns' and lies down on lap)
  - *crazy?* (hand makes large, erratic movements)

FOCUS
Newspaper Puppet

Use the newspaper to demonstrate how to create a puppet. Create a simple head and body shape by scrunching the paper at the top to form a head, the rest of the paper hangs below the head. There are a few simple 'rules' when working with puppets. These are known as The Three As:

Attention

When your puppet is talking or moving, pay attention to the puppet. This simply means you look at your puppet instead of the audience. If your attention is on the puppet, the audience's attention will be on the puppet. If your eye contact is on the audience, they will be looking at you instead of the puppet.

Articulation

This applies mainly to hand puppets (puppets that can move their mouth). When you open your mouth, the puppet opens their mouth. When your mouth is closed, the puppet's mouth is closed. If there are two syllables in a word, for example: 'hello', the puppet will begin with mouth closed, open for 'he', close briefly and open again for 'llo'. If your puppet has no moving mouthpart, they can 'bounce' as they talk.

Attitude

Give your puppet a different voice and way of speaking. This creates the illusion that the puppet has a 'life' of its own, that is separate from the puppeteer.

Sit the children as the audience. Stand or sit in front of the children. Perform a short and simple puppet show. You puppet show may go along the lines of:

PUPPET: Hello, my name is Flopsy.

CHILDREN: Hello!

PUPPET: How are you today?

CHILDREN: Good!

PUPPET: Would you like to see me dance?

CHILDREN: Yes!

PUPPET: Okay! Here I go!

The puppet dances and hums a tune.

After completing the performance, inform the children that they are now going to make their own puppets. Hand out a piece of newspaper to each child. When the children are ready, use the following instructions:

- *Are you ready to make your own puppet? I want you to remember that all our puppets are going to look very different.*

- *Can you try and twist or scrunch the paper to make a head?*

- *Good, now how will you create the body? You might like to tear or twist a section to make an arm. Just a few more moments working on your puppet.*

- *Great work, now it's time to bring your puppet to life.*

- *Let's all begin by putting our puppets to sleep. Good work, everyone.*

- *Can you make them move just a little bit like they are breathing? Do any of these puppets snore?*

- *Can you make your puppet:*
  - *yawn and stretch?*
  - *wash its face?*
  - *walk to the kitchen?*
  - *show that it is hungry (rub its tummy)?*
  - *eat?*
  - *dance?*
  - *wave 'hello' to the other puppets?*
  - *say 'goodbye'?*
  - *sleep?*

Depending on your group, either finish here or continue with the following:

- *Now let's find out a bit more about your puppet.*
- *Can you look at your puppet and think of a name?*
- *Now you need to find a voice for your puppet.*
- *We're going to practise all together.*
- *When I say go, can you please get your puppet to say, 'Hello, my name is _____.'*
- *Ready, go.*

All the children speak at the same time.

- *Good, now we are going to think of something that your puppet likes to do.*
- *For example: you might say, 'Hello, my name is Bobby, and I like to jump.'*
- *Let's all try together.*

All the children speak at the same time.

- *Great, now we are going to go around the circle and introduce our puppets one at a time.*

Go around the circle and give each child the opportunity to introduce his or her puppet. Remind the other children to sit quietly and respect each other as the puppets are presented.

- *Very good. Now we know a little bit more about these puppets.*
- *I think they are ready to find some new friends. Can you please turn to the person next to you and see if your puppets can have a little conversation together?*

Allow the class to spend a bit of time having a conversation between their puppets. Bring the class attention back and ask a pair of children to present their improvisation to the rest of the class.
Continue until all the children have had a turn.

FINISH
Puppet Song

Sing a few children's songs with the puppets such as 'Twinkle Twinkle Little Star' or 'ABC'. Remind the children that they need to keep the puppets moving as they 'sing' the words of the songs.

Extension

Sit the children in audience position. Set up a simple puppet theatre by placing two chairs in front of the audience. You may like to cover the chairs in fabric. Select two children at a time to present a small puppet show to the rest of the class. It might go something like:

The puppets enter.

PUPPET A: Hello.

PUPPET B: Hello.

PUPPET A: What's your name?

PUPPET B: My name is _____. What's your name?

PUPPET A: My name is _____ and I like to dance.

PUPPET B: Let's dance together.

They dance.

PUPPET A: That was fun, but I have to go. Goodbye.

PUPPET B: Goodbye.

The puppets exit.

Extracurricular Activities

- Invite the children to bring in puppets from home.
- Discuss the different kinds of puppets such as marionette, rod, glove and shadow puppets.
- Visit from or excursion to a puppet show.
- Explore shadow puppetry.
- See pages 116–17 for more activities.

Presenting Puppets

Resources

- Hand puppets, or a newspaper to make them.
- A large piece of fabric.
- Instrumental music.
- Two chairs.

WARM-UP
Puppet Voices

Ask the children to sit in a circle. When the students are settled, ask them to say 'good morning' then use the following instructions:

- *We're going to try lots of different ways to change our voice.*

- *Let's say 'good morning' again, but this time make your voice:*
  - *fast*
  - *slow*
  - *high*
  - *low*
  - *robotic*
  - *old*
  - *whisper*
  - *baby-like*
  - *scared*
  - *scary*
  - *loud*
  - *interesting*

Puppets

It is likely that you may have some hand puppets available at your centre to use for the following activity. If not, there are a number of ways to make simple hand puppets. There are some fabulous resources available on how to make sock puppets. For young children, this requires a bit more one-on-one attention, and you will also need to use a hot glue gun and wait for glue to dry completely before operating the puppets. However, the puppets look very effective and they can be used again and again. You can also use the newspaper puppets described in 'Making Puppets' (see pages 106–7) or give the children another piece of newspaper to create another puppet.

Puppetry Skills

Repeat the 'Puppet Emotion' exercise (see page 105) with the puppets you have selected to use.

Ask the children to decide on a name for their puppet. Sit the children in a circle and ask the puppets to introduce themselves to the rest of the group. Very young children may just say 'hello'. More confident children might say 'Hello, my name is _____.' Ask older children to share something about their puppet as part of the introduction. For example: 'Hello, my name is Mr Boggle, and I like to eat broccoli.'

FOCUS
Building a Puppet Character

- *We are going to create a character for our puppet.*
- *Let's start by experimenting with different voices for your puppet.*
- *Can you think of a voice that matches the look of your puppet?*
- *Can you decide on the thing your puppet likes to do most of all? For example: does your puppet like to:*
  - *eat chocolate?*
  - *go to the beach?*
  - *catch butterflies?*
  - *sing a song?*

Ask the children to sit in a circle and introduce their puppets using an interesting voice. After this, you may like to revise some of the puppetry skills from the previous lesson. For older children, in particular, if they are using a puppet with a moving mouth that can open and close, work on how to articulate words with their puppets. At the beginning and end of each word, and for most consonants, the mouth is closed. On the vowels and during each one-syllable word, the mouth is open. Remind the children that the puppeteer must always look at their puppet, not the audience. Explain that the audience focus will remain on the puppet as long as the puppeteer focuses on the puppet. Ask the children to experiment with different voices, but remind them that the puppet must speak slowly and clearly.

Performance

Divide the class into pairs. Ask the children to create a small puppet improvisation where the puppets enter the performance space, greet each other, talk about what they (the puppets) like or dislike, wave goodbye and exit. Once the children have rehearsed their scene, sit them in the audience position and create a simple puppet theatre in the performance space by placing two chairs in the centre of the stage and draping some fabric over the chairs.

The puppet conversation may look something like this:

PUPPET A: Hello.

PUPPET B: Hello.

PUPPET A: What's your name?

PUPPET B: _____. What's your name?

PUPPET A: _____. What do you like?

PUPPET B: I like _____. What do you like?

PUPPET A: I like _____. Would you like to play with me?

PUPPET B: Let's try jumping.

PUPPET A: Let's try flying.

PUPPET B: I liked playing with you.

The puppets hug.

PUPPET A: Goodbye.

PUPPET A *exits.*

PUPPET B: Goodbye!

PUPPET B *exits.*

For children who are reluctant to present work in front of their peers, ask them to create a scene where the puppets enter, wave, dance, hug each other, wave then exit. You might like to play some instrumental music in the background to create focus and keep the children engaged. Remind the children to applaud the performers after each performance.

FINISH
Puppet Musical Statues

Ask the children to find their own space in the room with their puppets. Play some music and ask the children to make their puppets dance. When the music stops, the children must freeze their puppets. You can either eliminate the children one by one, or find new ways for the puppets to freeze. For example: use levels or different positions when freezing: the puppets must freeze up high, the puppets must freeze down low, the puppets must freeze upside down, the puppets must freeze on the puppeteer's head, and so on.

Extension

Divide the class into pairs. Describe a simple improvisation for the students to try. You may like to try some of the following ideas, or ask the children to create their own:

- 'Have you seen my friend?' – Puppet A is asking the audience if they have seen Puppet B. Meanwhile, every time Puppet A exits or turns away, Puppet B appears.

- Running late – both puppets are running late. Puppet A is frantically trying to leave the 'house', meanwhile Puppet B keeps forgetting essential items. ('Wait! I forgot my lunch/hat/shoes.')

- Puppet argument – puppets have a disagreement about an issue, get mad at each other, then apologise and make up.

- Synchronised song – puppets sing and dance together. (Add a comedy element to this improvisation by getting Puppet A to fall asleep during the performance.)

Extracurricular Activities

- Make a puppet theatre using cardboard boxes. Children could work individually or in groups.

- Make and present finger puppets. Explore finger-play rhymes and songs.

- Host a puppet party and use playdough food or fake food from recycled materials.
- Make puppets from natural materials from outside.
- Discuss how puppets are used for storytelling around the world. Research together the history of puppetry.
- Draw a picture of your puppet. Write a story about your puppet's adventures.
- See page 109 for more activities.

Scarves

Resources

- A scarf (or a square metre of fabric in a light material) for each child.

WARM-UP
Ways of Moving

Ask the children to stand in a circle. When the children are ready, use the following instructions:

- *We are going to warm up our bodies in different ways.*

- *Can you make yourself as big as you can? Good, stretch right up.*

- *Now can you make yourself as small as you can? Good, crouch down as small as you can.*

- *Can you make yourself as wide as you can? Reach out as far as you can.*

- *Now let's see how flat you can be. Good work, you look like pancakes!*

- *Now can you stay in your spot and move your body fast?*

- *Good, now how slow can you move your body?*

- *Can you make your body look strong?*

- *Can you make your body look:*
  - *soft?*
  - *heavy?*
  - *light?*
  - *round?*
  - *straight?*
  - *like a zigzag?*

Emotion Hands

Ask the children to sit in a circle. When the students are settled, use the following instructions:

- *We are going to see if we can make our hands look different to how they are naturally. It might be a bit tricky, you might like to look at some of your friends to get some ideas.*

- *Can you make your hands look:*
  - *happy?*
  - *sad?*
  - *angry?*

- o *bored?*
- o *confused?*
- o *shy?*
- o *scared?*
- o *scary?*
- o *tired?*
- o *surprised?*
- o *silly?*
- o *sneaky?*

- *Well done, everyone, I saw lots of really good ideas.*

FOCUS

Playing with Scarves

Give each child a scarf. Ask them to find a space of their own to work in. When the children are ready, use the following instructions:

- *Let's play with our scarves and see what they can do.*

- *Can you make your scarf:*
  - big?
  - small?
  - flat?
  - wide?
  - fast?
  - slow?
  - strong?
  - soft?
  - heavy?
  - light?
  - round?
  - straight?

Emotions

Explain that it is good to try new things and new colours. Use the following instructions:

- *I want to see now if we can make our scarves show different emotions or feelings. It might be a bit tricky, so it's okay to have a look at other people's ideas if you get stuck.*

- *Can you make your scarf look:*
  - happy?
  - sad?
  - angry?
  - bored?
  - confused?
  - shy?
  - scared?
  - scary?
  - tired?
  - surprised?
  - silly?
  - sneaky?

Character

When the children are settled, use the following instructions:

- *You are doing such a great job, everyone. We're going to see how these scarves might be used to help us become different characters.*

- *This time, use your scarf as a costume to help you become a fairy. Very good, I like the way you are using your scarf to look like wings.*

- *We're going to try some more characters.*

- *Are you ready? How might you use your scarf to pretend you are:*
  - *a robot?*
  - *an alien?*
  - *a king?*
  - *a monster?*
  - *a cowboy?*
  - *a baby?*
  - *a witch?*
  - *an old lady?*
  - *a waiter?*

Transformation

Use the following instructions:

- *You are doing such a great job! I am going to make it even trickier now because you are all so clever.*

- *Now we are going to turn our scarves into different objects. Let's try the first one. Can you turn your scarf into:*
  - *a hat?*
  - *a shoe?*
  - *a necklace?*
  - *a baby?*
  - *a pillow?*
  - *a wall?*
  - *a telephone?*
  - *a trampoline?*
  - *a belt?*
  - *a horse?*
  - *a motorbike?*
  - *a bag?*

- *Great work! You are all doing such a wonderful job transforming your scarves!*

From here you might like to divide the class into two groups. Group 1 becomes the audience and Group 2 the performers. Sit Group 1 in the audience position. Ask Group 2 to spread out and face the audience. Repeat some of the exercises from above. After maybe five to eight instructions, ask Group 2 to take a bow. Remind Group 1 to give the performers a round of applause. Swap groups and repeat the exercise with different instructions.

Presenting

Ask the children to sit in a circle or in the audience position. Select 2 or 3 children at a time to enter the performance space and ask them to use the scarf as one of the emotions, objects or characters from the lists above. You might like to encourage the children to present their demonstrations individually, but if they resist, allow them to present as pairs or in groups of 3. Ask the audience to try and guess what the presentations are. For very young children, whisper a suggestion for them to try. Repeat until all the children have presented. Remind the children to give the performers a round of applause when they have finished performing.

FINISH
Sleeping Scarves

Ask the children to scrunch their scarves in a tight little ball and, on your command, throw them into the air and try to catch them. Repeat 3–4 times. Then ask the children to scrunch their scarf into a teeny tiny ball again. Ask them to whisper a little thank you to their scarf. Tell the children that the scarves are tired and need a rest. Ask the children to bring the scarves to you and collect them in a basket or box.

Extension

Divide the class into groups of 3–5. Give each child a scarf. Ask them to improvise a scene where the scarf must transform at least three times. Either give the whole class a setting or give each group a different place. The settings might include:

o a picnic when a storm comes
o a haunted house when a ghost appears
o a hat or handbag shop with a fussy customer
o a fancy restaurant with a meal disaster
o a bank during a robbery

Give the class 5 minutes to prepare. Seat the class in the audience position and then ask the groups to present their scenes one at a time. Ensure the actors take a bow at the end and the audience gives them a round of applause.

Two Characters Meeting

Divide the children into pairs – ask them to use the scarf to become a character from the character list above or to think up one of their own. Ask each pair to improvise a meeting between their two characters. Suggest the meeting takes place in a park, a restaurant or a shop. Allow all the pairs to work at the same time and then call 'freeze' and show some of the work. Encourage the children to speak loudly, show facial expression and use interesting gestures to portray their characters.

Keep the improvisations short. For example: two children might have chosen to be a monster and an old lady:

LADY: What a nice day at the park.

MONSTER: Rarghhh!

LADY: Who are you?

MONSTER: I'm a monster.

LADY: What do you want?

MONSTER: I want to eat you!

Another example might be a princess and a waiter:

WAITER: What would you like?

PRINCESS: I'll have a cup of tea.

WAITER (*miming serving tea*): There you go.

PRINCESS: Thank you.

WAITER (*spilling the tea*): Oh, I'm very sorry.

PRINCESS: You have ruined my dress!

Children might like to present a scene as the same character, for example: two pirates at sea, two witches creating a magic potion.

Extracurricular Activities

- Lay out all the scarves and discuss the different colours and patterns.
- Play musical mats.
- Peg the scarves together on a string or rope and hang them across your room.
- Wrap some dolls or toys with the scarves to imitate wrapping a baby.
- Discuss how scarves are used as costumes and how they are worn in traditional dress around the world.
- Have a 'wear a scarf to class' day.
- Cut out pictures from old newspapers and magazines of people wearing scarves.

Paint a Picture

Resources

- Instrumental music (optional).
- Images of paintings from a variety of artists and mediums.
- Patterned scarves or squares of fabric.

WARM-UP
Finger Painting

Ask the children to sit in a circle. When the children are settled, use the following instructions:

- *We are going to warm up our fingers and hands.*
- *Can you show me your hands?*
- *Stretch out your fingers.*
- *Shake your hands.*
- *Can you make your hands look big?*
- *Can you make your hands look small?*
- *Can you make your hands move up high?*
- *Can you make your hands come down flat?*
- *Let's imagine that we are holding a paintbrush.*
- *We are going to draw a face.*

Mime painting a picture of a face in the air in front of you with the class.

- *Can you paint the parts as I describe them?*
- *Let's start with a big round circle.*
- *Let's paint the eyes.*
- *Can you paint a nose?*
- *Let me see you paint a mouth.*
- *Now it is time to paint the ears.*
- *Finally, let's paint the hair.*
- *Great work. Now let's decorate the rest of the painting with some spots.*

Painting the Space

Ask the children to stand in a circle. When the children are ready, use the following instructions:

- *Let's imagine that our feet are like big paintbrushes.*
- *Imagine we have just stepped into a big puddle of paint.*
- *Let's walk our footprints all around the space. Cover as much of the floor as you can.*

Encourage the children to walk in all directions around the space. Remind them that there is no running or touching anybody else.

- *What colour are your footprints?*
- *Let's dip our feet into the paint again, but this time use a different colour.*
- *Let's see what other patterns you can make with your feet paintbrushes.*
- *Can you change the way you walk to create different patterns and lines?*
- *Well done, everyone. Freeze.*
- *Great work, have a look at our floor. It looks fantastic.*
- *Now let's turn our hands and fingers into paintbrushes and paint the air.*
- *Dip your finger paintbrush into some paint. Let's paint some big spots all around the room.*
- *Can you show me how you paint:*
  - *high?*
  - *low?*
  - *small?*
  - *big?*
  - *fast?*
  - *slow?*
  - *on your body?*
  - *on your hair?*
- *Now we are going to use our whole bodies as a paintbrush. Dip yourself into a different colour.*
- *What sorts of patterns and shapes can you paint with your whole body?*

It is optional here to play some appropriate instrumental music and allow the children to explore painting the space. Encourage large, slow movements. Remind the children to use their whole body to paint, rather than just their hands and fingers.

- *Excellent work. Now let's fill the space with some big stripes.*
- *Try to use a different body part for each stripe you paint.*

Discuss

Ask the children to sit in a circle. When the children are settled, ask them to observe each other and look around the room and identify anyone wearing something with either spots or stripes; or any posters, furniture or objects that have spots or stripes. Show the children a selection of famous paintings and ask them to identify any spots or stripes they can see in them. After they have identified the spots and stripes, ask the children what other shapes they can see in the paintings.

FOCUS
Making a Painting

Select one of the paintings either by voting with the children or by choosing one as the teacher. Ask the children to sit in the audience position. Explain that the performance space is going to be our blank canvas and that we are going to use our bodies to paint the space. Look at the painting again, and as a whole class, identify the main shapes, figures and characteristics of the painting.

Select some children to enter the performance space and use their bodies to copy or communicate the painting. For some paintings, the children will be able to identify and copy people, buildings or animals. For others, those with no figures, the children's interpretations will become more abstract.

Continue with different pieces of art, ensuring that everyone has an opportunity to present and also to observe their peers at work.

You may want to 'bring the art to life' after the children are in position. Ask them to hold their positions in a freeze, then clap your hands and ask them to 'come to life' for a few moments (maybe 10 seconds) then ask them to return to the freeze position.

FINISH
Spots and Stripes

Spread out some of the coloured and patterned scarves around the room. Play some music and ask the children to dance around the space. When the music stops, call out 'spots' or 'stripes' (or any other pattern or colour of the scarves). Children must try to stand on or near the scarf that matches the teacher's direction.

Obstacle Course

Using wool, ribbon or rope, create a continuous line that the children can walk on and follow. Include zigzags, wavy lines, right angles, spirals and circles to jump in. For older children, make the course harder by adding obstacles, such as chairs to step over, balancing planks, hoops to go through or poles to walk under. Ask the children to identify the shapes and patterns. Be sure to mark the start and finish of the obstacle course clearly. Send the children through the course one at a time or in 10-second intervals, depending on the age and the size of your space. Repeat using a new pattern and course. Encourage good balancing, jumping skills, concentration and focus.

Extension

Ask the children to identify as many animals as they can which have particular patterns and markings. Divide the class into small groups and ask them to present a small scene about one of the animals they have identified for example: 'How the zebra got its stripes' or 'How the leopard got its spots'. Ask them to include the role of a narrator and encourage the children to face the audience and to speak loudly and clearly.

Extracurricular Activities

- Draw a picture of yourself and decorate with spots, stripes and other patterns.

- Discuss patterns and animals. Why do some animals have particular markings?

- Have a spots-and-stripes day – wear patterned clothes to class.

- Read the *Spot* book series by Eric Hill.

- Bring something patterned to class.

- Have a zoo excursion and identify animals with spots or stripes.

- Draw patterns in the sand, indoors on a sand table or outdoors in the sandpit.

- Make patterns in playdough or clay.

- Use famous pieces of art as a starting point for drawing, painting or sculpture experiences.

- Discuss and identify famous artists and their work.

- Have an art exhibition.

- Identify different colours and collect objects from each colour to display.

THREE

PLACES AND ANIMALS

The Beach

Resources

- Some scarves, or small squares of fabric (optional).
- A long piece of blue fabric.
- Relaxation music.
- Some little shells or star-shaped sequins (optional).

WARM-UP
Waves

Ask the children to stand in a circle holding hands.
Remind the children that they should be respectful
of each other and not pull on each other's arms and
hands. When the children are settled use the
following instructions:

- *Let's make our circle smaller by coming in towards
  the middle.*
- *Good, now let's make it bigger by moving back.*
- *Good work, I like the way you aren't pulling on your
  friend's hands. Remember, we're not falling over.*
- *Let's do it again! In we go.*
- *Good now back again.*
- *Now as we move in, can you make the sound
  'shhh'?*
- *Good, work everyone. Ready?*

Repeat two or three times. Make the sound 'shhh'
as you move in towards the centre.

- *What does that sound like?*

Allow the children to offer their answers. They
should come to the conclusion that it sounds like
waves.

- *Yes, that's right, it sounds like waves.*
- *Let's gently drop each other's hands now.*
- *As we move into the centre, can you raise your
  arms like the big waves of the ocean?*

Repeat.

- *Where do we see waves?*

Allow the children to offer their answers. They
should come to the conclusion that you see big
waves at the beach.

- *That's right, at the beach! Well guess what? We are
  going to the beach today.*
- *We have to get ready. Get your beach bag.*
- *What do we need to take to the beach?*

Listen to the children's ideas and repeat some of
them as you pack the bag.

- *Let's put these items into our beach bag.*

Mime putting the items into your 'bag'. Some suggestions include:

- o towel
- o swimming costume
- o sunscreen
- o hat
- o bucket and spade (beach toys)
- o snacks
- o drinks

FOCUS
A Day at the Beach

Ask the children to stand next to their 'beach bag'. When the children are ready, use the following instructions:

- *Okay, I think we're ready to have a day at the beach.*
- *Pick up your bags, are they heavy?*
- *Let's walk to the beach. It's a bit of a long walk to the beach. We have to start by walking up this big hill!*

Explore different ways of walking (hot, thirsty, tired walking or excited quick steps), crossing roads, walking up and down hills, getting hot, passing the shops before eventually arriving at the beach. When you arrive suggest the following actions and mime together with the children.

- *Okay, we're here.*
- *Put down your bag.*
- *Take off your shoes.*
- *Spread out your towel* (you can use scarves or just mime this).
- *We've already got our swimming costumes on under our clothes, so let's take off our tops.*
- *Let's put some sunscreen on.*
- *Can you open up your bag and have a cool drink?*
- *Let's walk on the sand. Can you feel the sand in between your toes? Pick up some sand and let it run through your hands.*
- *I think I'm ready to test the water. Let's walk down to the edge of the waves.*

Line the children up along one side of the room. Stretch out the long piece of blue fabric along the floor to represent the water. Hold one end and ask an assistant to hold the other. (If you don't have an assistant, ask one of the children.) 'Snake' the fabric forward and backward like the waves at the shore. Ask the children to come close to the water's edge without getting their feet wet.

- *Well done! I think you might be ready for a little swim.*

Line the children along one side of the room. Now spread the fabric out on the floor. Ask the children to step 'into the water'.

- *Can you feel the cool water and soft sand underneath you?*

- *Let's go out a bit deeper. Can you imagine you are wading in deeper water?*

- *Let's play in the waves. Can you splash about in the waves?*

- *Let's imagine we are holding our breath so we can swim underwater.*

Ask the children to step off the fabric for a moment. Hold up one end and ask an assistant (or one of the children) to hold up the other end. Raise it over the children's heads and invite them to swim deeper 'underwater'.

- *Let's put our goggles on and explore under the water.*

Allow the children some time to explore under the water.

- *Let's come up for a breath of air.*

Lower the fabric down one side of the group.

- *What did you see when you went swimming underwater? Did you see any fish, seaweed or shells?*

- *Take a big breath and let's go under the water again.*

Continue exploring under the water. You may want to play the relaxation music as the children are swimming. Encourage the children to remain silent throughout this experience and 'do their own work' rather than follow or copy other children.

- *I think we have had enough swimming now. You must be getting tired.*

Lower the fabric and remove it.

- *Let's come back to the warm sand. Shall we build a sandcastle?*

Allow the children time to mime building a sandcastle. They may choose to build on their own, work in small groups or work together as a whole class.

- *Let's decorate it now. Who can find a shell? What colour is yours? Is it big or small? Does it have any patterns? Can you find a space of your own to build a sandcastle?*

Ask the children to build their own sandcastle then jump on it.

- *Oh look, our hands are all sandy. Let's rinse them in the sea.*
- *Come and sit down now on your towels.*
- *Shall we eat our sandwich now?* (Mime eating.)
- *What a busy day we've had at the beach.*
- *Let's all lie down on our towels.*

Stretch the fabric out and hold one end. Use an assistant (or select a child to hold the other end) and hold the fabric over the children, who are lying down, gently lifting the fabric up and down to create 'waves'. Play some relaxation music, and ask the children to remember their favourite part of their visit to the beach. Ask the children to close their eyes while they remember the trip. Take the fabric away and sprinkle little shell sequins or little stars around the space. Ask the children to open their eyes and see if they can find their own treasure from the beach.

Extension

Brainstorm with the children and write a list of possible 'disasters' that may occur at the beach. Encourage exaggerated and implausible scenarios to keep things light and add a comedic element. Ideas could include:

- a giant octopus attacks the family
- a pirate treasure chest is discovered and pirates battle with the beachgoers
- a beach becomes overcrowded by a crab invasion.

Divide the class into small groups and give them time to improvise their scene. Sit the class in audience position and show each group's work.

Extracurricular Activities

- Sand play and sandcastles. Bury shells in the sandpit for the children to find. Use a sieve to separate shells, sand and pebbles.

- An excursion to the beach.

- Play beach volleyball or beach cricket outside.

- Play with a giant inflatable beach ball.

- Make a class beach using fabric, fishing nets and paper cut-outs. Play appropriate beach or holiday music.

- Bring in favourite holiday photos of beaches.

- Discuss responsible beach habits (such as no littering, sun protection and not swimming out of your depth) and environmental impacts.

- Read stories set on or near a beach.

The Circus

Resources

- Circus music.
- A hoop.
- Some coloured scarves or a selection of brightly coloured costumes.
- A rope, string or chalk to mark out a circle, or a parachute.
- A drum (optional).

WARM-UP
Follow the Leader

Begin by asking the children to walk around the space. Remind the children that there is no running and no touching anybody else. When the children are engaged in the warm-up, use the following instructions:

- *Let's see if you can walk in different directions, not just around and around in a circle. Good.*

- *As you are walking, see if you can start following someone in the room. Don't let them see you! If that person catches you following them, you must follow someone else. Quick, check if you are being followed! Turn around. Good, continue on.*

- *Can you follow somebody else now?*

- *Let's try to work in different ways to music.*

- *Play the circus music in the background.*

- *Can you balance on one leg? Try the other one. Good work!*

- *Let's all line up on this side of the room.*

- *I'm going to lay this hoop in the centre here. When you get to the hoop, can you jump into it, then jump back out again?*

Ask each of the children to take it in turns to walk up to the hoop, jump into it and out again, then rejoin the back of the line.

- *Well done, everyone! I'm going to hold the hoop like this* (hold the hoop so that it just touches the ground).

- *See if you can crawl through the hoop when you come to it.*

Ask each of the children to take it in turns to walk up to the hoop, crawl through the hoop then rejoin the back of the line. After each of the children have crawled through the hoop, ask the children to sit in a circle.

- *Excellent! Can anybody hula hoop?*

Select some children to come into the centre and hula hoop. Remind the children to applaud the performers after each attempt at hula hooping.

- *Good work, everyone! Now our bodies are warmed up.*
- *But what about our faces? Now let's try some silly faces.*

Sit the children in a circle and ask them to make a funny face. Children can try some of their own, or you can ask the children to turn to the person next to them and copy each other's funny faces.

Character

Explore the following characters together with the class. Ensure that there is no touching, pushing or running. Spend 30–60 seconds on each character. Again, have the circus music playing in the background.

- *Let's all be:*
  - o *a clown* (funny faces, crazy walks, falling down, funny dancing)
  - o *an acrobat* (tumbling and rolling, interesting balances and shapes)
  - o *a dancer* (spinning, twirling, graceful movements and gestures)
  - o *a lion tamer* (cracking a whip, careful movements, brave poses)
  - o *a tightrope walker* (balancing along a line which can be drawn in chalk, marked out with a rope or imaginary)
  - o *a strong man* (lifting weights, muscle poses)
  - o *a lion* (fierce faces, jumping through hoops, jumping on and off a chair)
  - o *a horse* (gallop in a circle, change direction, precise feet movements)

Chorus

In drama a chorus is a group of actors who say the same thing at the same time. It is a good way to encourage children who are reluctant to present work on their own to speak out loud. A chorus can also involve the group making the same actions at the same time.

Teach the children the following chorus. Encourage loud, clear voices and lots of gestures with their hands as they deliver the lines:

- 'Roll up! Roll up! Come on down!'
- 'The greatest circus is in town!'

Repeat until the children are confident of remembering the lines. Ask them to finish the chorus with an interesting 'circus' pose. This may be arms up, or one arm up and one arm out. It may be kneeling on one knee.

Discuss

Remain in the circle and discuss the circus with the children. You may wish to ask questions such as:

- *Who has ever been to the circus?*
- *What did you see?*
- *Have you seen a picture in a book or seen something on TV about a circus?*
- *What do you know about the circus?*
- *What do you think happens at the circus?*

FOCUS
The Circus Has Come to Town

Give each of the children a piece of costume or a scarf. If you are using scarves, they can be worn any way they like: as a cape, around the head, around the neck, tied around one leg, tucked in the back as a tail, around the waist and so forth.

Either draw a large circle in the centre of the room with chalk, or define the space with a rope or string. Explain to the children that this will be their circus ring. If your centre has a parachute, use this. Establish an offstage position. The teacher must now assume the role of the Ringmaster, but be ready to switch back to give further instructions as needed.

Stand the children in a line waiting for their introduction. If your group is very large, ask half of the children to sit as the audience.

> RINGMASTER: Roll up! Roll up! Ladies and gentleman, boys and girls. Prepare to be amazed and entertained by the spectacular, the colourful, the talented... CIRCUS PARADE!

Play the circus music. Ask all the children to circle the ring then spread out to find a position on their own. Use a drum or a visual cue for the children to get into their most interesting circus position.

> RINGMASTER: And now, ladies and gentleman, get ready for the funny, the kooky, the hilarious, CRAZY CLOWNS!

> TEACHER: Okay, everyone, let's all follow around the ring as the clowns. Show me your funny walks.

All the children enter as clowns. For older children, give them time to prepare a funny clown act, for example: coming in together and falling backwards with their legs in the air.

> RINGMASTER: And now let's say goodbye to the clowns. Give them a round of applause.

> TEACHER: Okay, let's move out of the ring. We are going to become a different circus character now. Ready?

RINGMASTER: And now, ladies and gentleman, please welcome the amazing acrobats. Here they come into the ring, watch their amazing balances and tricks.

Continue in this way with all the other circus characters. You can make the acts as simple or as detailed as you like, depending on the age and sophistication of your group. Try dividing the class into groups of characters and establish a running order, so that each group knows when to perform. Encourage the children to perform out to the front and ask the rest of the class to applaud each act. If there is no audience, place some empty chairs and ask the children to imagine the audience and direct their performance and acting to the chairs.

RINGMASTER: And now it's time to say goodbye to all the fabulous fun of the circus. Please welcome to the ring for the final time, the circus performers!

Repeat the parade, then ask the children to exit the circus ring.

If you have one group of children as the audience, swap the groups and repeat the activity. If you divided the class into groups of characters, and time permits, rotate the characters.

Play music and ask the children to move and dance. When the music stops the children must freeze in a circus-character position. Congratulate the children on using good facial expressions and thinking of different circus characters.

Extension

Divide the class into small groups and ask them to develop a short circus act. Ideas include magic tricks, acrobats, balancing acts, jokes or animal acts. Give them time to prepare and rehearse their act, then take on the role of Ringmaster and create a whole-class circus show. Begin with the 'Roll up, roll up!' chorus above and incorporate each group in turn.

Extracurricular Activities

- Have a 'crazy hair' day.
- Make popcorn.
- Make tickets for the show. Invite other classes, parents or teachers to watch the show. Decorate the room in bright colours. Drape fabric from the walls to the centre of the room to create a 'big top'.
- Practise tumbles and somersaults on gym mats.
- Ask the children to paint or draw a clown face or their favourite circus character.
- Bring face paints to class. Let the children work on each other!
- Circus excursion or circus-skills workshops.
- Find out some historical facts about the circus, and circuses around the world.
- Create circus props from recycled materials.
- Read books about the circus or circus characters.

The Farm

Resources

- Several coloured pieces of fabric.
- Some plastic farm animals or pictures of farm animals.

WARM-UP
Statues

Ask the children to stand in a circle. When the children are settled, use the following instructions:

- *I am going to ask you to make some statues. Remember, statues don't move and they don't make a sound.*

- *Ready? Can you make a BIG statue?*

- *Good, now I'm going to give you just a few seconds to make a SMALL statue. Oh wow! There are some very tiny statues here.*

- *Now try a WIDE statue. Good, I like the way you are really stretching.*

- *Next one is a THIN statue. Good, I like the way you aren't moving at all.*

- *Now can you make a statue of someone very, very YOUNG. I like the way you are using your faces. Remember, no sound.*

- *And the last one. Can you make an OLD statue? Look at those crooked backs and wrinkly faces. You do look old!*

- *And relax, let's sit down where you are.*

Song

- *I know someone old. He wears overalls, he has a big straw hat and he rides a tractor.*

- *And do you know where he lives?*

- *He lives on a farm. It's called Old MacDonald's Farm.*

- *Can you show me a statue of Old MacDonald?*

Allow the children time to move into a position of Old MacDonald.

- *Now when I clap my hands, he is going to come to life.*

- *Show me how he walks.*

- *Can you say 'good morning' like Old MacDonald?*

• *Good, do you know the song about Old MacDonald?*

Sing through four or five verses of 'Old MacDonald had a Farm' with the children. Ask them to explore each animal's movement and sound. The children switch between walking in character as Old MacDonald and becoming the animal.

Discuss

All stories have a problem (conflict) to make them interesting.

• *Can you think of an idea for a problem at the farm?*

All stories have an ending.

• *How can we end this story?*

• *And how might we fix this problem?*

18

FOCUS
Our Farm Story

Ask the children to sit in a circle and make a list of all the animals they can think of that live on a farm. If anyone suggests an animal that doesn't live on a farm, for example: a tiger or an elephant, try to identify where that animal does belong. Once the children have exhausted the list of possible animals, use the following instructions with the children:

- *We are going to make up our very own story about a farm.*

- *First, we need some characters.*

- *What animals shall we put into our story?*

Encourage the children to come up with a list of characters for the story. Try to keep it to a maximum of five characters to avoid possible confusion. If the children do not nominate a farmer, discuss the importance of having a farmer with the children and decide if you need one or not.

Record the children's ideas as they come. All children should be encouraged to participate, without losing the momentum of the story. Keep the story simple and short. If there are lots of ideas, advise the children that those ideas will be used another time.

Divide the class into groups and use pieces of fabric to help define the space. Nominate particular pieces as the stable, pen, paddock and so forth. Tell the story that the children have developed and allow the children to act it out. It might be something like:

- *Once upon a time, there was a farmer. And every morning, he woke up and had to feed the animals. First he went to the pigs. He said 'good morning, pigs', and he gave them some carrots. Then he went to the hens and collected the warm eggs. (Continue.) But one day, when he got to the stable, he realised the horse was gone!*

Continue to narrate the story and allow the children to act it out. If your class is large, set up half the group as an audience and rotate them. Encourage the 'actors' to take a bow and the audience to give them a round of applause after the performance.

FINISH

You will need a collection of toy farm animals or pictures of farm animals. Sit the children in a circle or in the audience position. Select a child to choose one of the animals, enter the performance space and pretend to be that animal. The audience must try to guess the animal. Repeat until all the children have had a turn.

Create paddocks by spreading out some scarves or large pieces of material around the space. Play some music and call out a farm animal. The children have to pretend to be the animal until the music stops. The children must return to a paddock and wait for the music to start again, and the next animal is called out.

Extension

Divide the class into groups of 3–5. Ask the children to nominate one person to be the narrator. Each group must present a scene called 'The Surprise'. Each scene must be set on a farm. Give the children 5–10 minutes to prepare their scene. Then sit the class as an audience and present the groups one at a time.

Extracurricular Activities

- Sheep picture – draw a paddock and stick on cotton wool balls for a sheep. Draw legs and a head.
- Discuss the production of milk and milk products.
- Farm excursion.
- Living eggs programme – children watch and learn about the cycle of eggs, chicks and hens.
- Draw or paint your favourite farm animal.
- Create a story about your own farm.
- Discuss the different kinds of farms, including the produce they sell.
- Make a farmer's garden – create a vegetable patch.
- Read and discuss books about farm animals or farm production.

The Jungle

Resources

- A drum.
- A tambourine or rainstick.
- Relaxation music.
- Jungle sound effects or music.

WARM-UP
Moving to the Drum

Ask the children to find their own space in the room. Use a drum, or something similar, to beat out a simple rhythm for the children to march to. Let the children explore walking in time to the beat. Once the children have had time exploring the beat, use the following instructions:

- *When I play the drum very loud like this, can you find a way to walk?*
- *And when I play it very softly like this, can you find a new way to walk?*
- *What about when I play it very fast?*
- *What about when I play it very slow?*
- *Excellent work finding different ways of moving!*
- *Now I'm going to keep playing the drum and change the volume and the speed of the drumming.*
- *Are you ready? The drumming is going to change a lot.*
- *Be ready to change the way you move.*

Alternate the tempo (speed) from fast to slow. Experiment with the volume to include soft and loud beats.

Discuss

Ask the children to sit in a circle and discuss what they know about a jungle.

- *What does a jungle look like?*
- *What do the plants and vegetation look like?*
- *What do you know about the jungle?*

The children's responses will vary and may include such things as strange flowers, spiky plants, long vines and tall trees. You may also want to show the children some images of jungles from around the world.

Trees

Ask the children to find a space of their own. When the children are settled in their own space, use the following instructions:

- *Can you crouch down in a tiny shape? I can see so many tiny shapes!*

- *I am going to shake the tambourine (or rainstick). When I make this sound I am going to count down slowly from ten to one. As I slowly count down from ten to one can you grow into the shape of an interesting tree or plant? Excellent work! I can see so many interesting trees and plants!*

- *This time, as I slowly count from one to ten, can you shrink back down into your tiny shape?*

Repeat.

Jungle Picture

Divide the class into two groups. Ask one group to sit on the audience mat. Ask the other group to find a space of their own, and face the audience in a tiny shape. Shake the tambourine and count down from ten to one. Ask the children to grow into a 'jungle' shape as the audience observes the jungle picture. Repeat the exercise and encourage shapes to join together, asymmetrical shapes and interesting use of levels. Swap the groups over, so the original audience creates the picture and the other group becomes the audience. Remind the children to applaud the performers at the end of each performance.

Discuss

Ask the children to sit in a circle and discuss what they know about animals that live in a jungle. If someone suggests an animal that doesn't live in the jungle, for example: a cow or a guinea pig, ask the children where it actually belongs.

FOCUS
A Jungle Journey

Ask the children to find their own space in the room. When the children are settled, use the following instructions:

- *We are going to the jungle today! First we have to get ready.*
- *Let's put on our explorer clothes.* (Mime putting on the clothes.)
- *What else should we wear to protect us?*

Allow the children to call out different answers such as shoes, a hat or a jacket. Mime putting on each item.

- *Let's get our backpacks.* (Mime.)
- *What does an explorer need to take to the jungle?*

Use the children's ideas to put things into the backpack. Mime each item as you go. Suggestions could include a water bottle, some food, mosquito repellent, a camera, binoculars, a tent and a torch.

- *Okay, brave explorers, we are ready to go.*
- *Let's get our binoculars out.*
- *Have you got your cameras? Let's make sure they work. Click!*
- *Come on, brave explorers, let's begin our jungle adventure.*

Sing the following song as you move around the space:

- 'Walking through the jungle, what do I see?'

Children move around with 'binoculars'.

- 'I can see a... parrot squawking at me.'

Children turn into parrots, mimicking sound and movements. Repeat with:

- o 'a snake slithering around me'
- o 'a tiger growling at me'
- o 'a crocodile snapping at me'
- o 'some insects scurrying about me'
- o 'some monkeys chattering in the trees'

After 'seeing' each animal, ask the children to return to being explorers. As explorers, the children should take a photo of the animal and record some information about it in their 'explorer journal'. Mime writing information into a mimed book, such as 'We saw a parrot high in the trees.'

Throughout this experience, you might like to 'camp' in the jungle. Ask the children to pitch the tent and set up a campfire. Open your backpacks and mime eating some food. Gather the children together and ask them to roll out their sleeping bags. Ask them to close their eyes and listen to the sounds of the jungle. You might like to play some appropriate relaxation music or sound effects. Wake the children up, and ask them to prepare for the next day of exploring. You may choose to end the class here, or continue with the following activities.

Animal Movement Piece

Play the jungle music softly in the background. Ask the children to spread out and find a place to stand on their own. Remind the children not to run or touch anyone else during the activity. When the children are settled, use the following instructions:

- *Can you show me a statue of a large, colourful bird?*

- *When I shake the tambourine, can you bring your bird to life?*

Allow the children a few moments to explore bringing the animal to life.

- *Freeze.*

- *This time when I shake the tambourine, can you make your birds by just using your face and bodies, without any sound?*

- *Well done, everyone! I can see some great birds.*

- *Can you make you your movements even bigger?*

Children move around the space in mime. Repeat this activity with other jungle animals.

Jungle Movement

Place some scarves or mats around a central performing area. Divide the class into small groups and allocate a different jungle animal to each group. Sit each group on a different scarf or mat. Create a movement piece to music. Your finished piece could go something like:

- Children spread out in the centre and get down low into a small 'seed shape'.

- Children slowly grow into the jungle. (Count down from ten to one.)

- Children move to their mats.

Each group takes it in turns to come into the centre, mime their creature and return to the mat. These may include:

  o monkeys
  o snakes
  o tigers
  o insects

- All children enter the space and move around together.

- All return to a frozen jungle position then shrink to a small shape.

Repeat with different characters. Repeat with half of the group performing and the other half as the audience. Swap over.

FINISH

Discuss how people used to communicate to each other by sending messages on drums. Sit the children in a circle. Play some simple rhythms on the drum and ask the children to copy by clapping out the same rhythm on their knees. After several rhythms, select one of the children to be the leader. Repeat the activity using another child as the leader.

Extension

Divide the class into small groups and ask them to create a short movement sequence about the jungle. Insist that there is no sound or narration. They must communicate their story or presentation in mime – relying only on their facial expressions, gesture and body movements.

Extracurricular Activities

- Make a snake by drawing a spiral onto a square of paper. Decorate and cut out.

- Make drums from empty containers, tins and other recycled materials. Make drumsticks with chopsticks, small garden stakes or kebab skewers with a bead on the end.

- Create a jungle mural. Use leaf cut-outs or attach vegetation from outside. Finish with animals.

- Make a jungle in the sandpit by using sticks, branches and leaves. Decorate with plastic jungle animals.

- Go on an excursion to the zoo – identify the animals that live in the jungle.

- Environmental discussion – discuss the importance of protecting wildlife and habitat.

- Make a jungle mask – decorate with feathers, scraps of material and textured papers.

- Enact the story 'Five Little Monkeys'.

The Restaurant

Resources

- Chairs or scarves to sit on.
- An apron for teacher in role (optional).
- Chairs for the restaurant.
- Costumes and a few props for the restaurant, such as a handbag, a wooden spoon or a bowl (optional).

WARM-UP
Something with Something

Ask the children to find their own space in the room. Remind the children that they should not run or touch anybody else. When the students are settled, use the following instructions:

- *Let's all walk around the space.*
- *When I call 'freeze', you are going to be a still as a statue. Ready? Freeze. Excellent work.*
- *Let's move around the space again. This time when I call 'freeze', I am going to ask you to touch something with the body part that I call out. Ready? Freeze.*
- *Can you touch something green with your toe? Good!*
- *Back to your natural walk.*
- *Freeze!*
- *Can you touch something hard with your hand? Good work.*
- *I like the way you're listening and being careful of each other.*

Try a whole range of textures, colours and surfaces.

- *Can you touch:*
  - *something wooden with your elbow?*
  - *something pink with your head?*
  - *the middle of the room with your bottom?*
  - *the carpet with your ear?*

Mime

Ask the children to sit in a circle. When the children are settled, ask them to mime the following actions:

- eat wiggly noodles with a fork
- lick a big ice cream
- eat a crunchy biscuit
- sip some soup from a spoon

Place chairs or scarves around the room and ask the children to sit on them. Once the children are settled, ask them use big facial expressions while eating something:

- o yummy
- o yucky
- o in tiny pieces
- o hot and spicy
- o hard
- o big
- o slimy and slippery
- o smelly
- o that you have never tried – but you think it is delicious!

Discuss

Ask the children to sit in a circle and discuss what they know about restaurants.

- *Do you know what a restaurant is?*
- *Who has been to a restaurant?*
- *Who was with you?*
- *What did you order?*
- *What do you like eat at a restaurant?*
- *Who knows what we call the person who takes the orders?*

FOCUS
Teacher in Role

Ask the children to sit in a circle. Explain that you are going pretend to be the waiter or waitress.

Turn away from the children and assume the role. You might like to tie an apron around yourself to help you get into role. You will need to switch from your role back to yourself as a teacher throughout the activity.

The children will also be switching characters from customers to the chef.

> WAITRESS: Hello and welcome to the _____ restaurant. I will be your waitress for this morning (afternoon) and the specials today are _____ and _____. (*To one of the children.*) Hello, can I take your order?
>
> *Child gives the order.*
>
> Excellent choice. And what would you like, sir?

Continue taking orders from the whole class. Be sure to be only a few seconds with each child. If the children begin to get restless, explain the 'rules of the restaurant' – no running around, calling out, etc.

> TEACHER: What happens once the waitress has taken all the orders? Where does she go?
>
> CHILDREN: To the kitchen.

Prompt the children to identify the role of the chef.

> TEACHER: Come on, let's all be chefs in the kitchen. We need to chop, slice, cut, stir, mix.

The children mime these actions.

> TEACHER: Quick! Back to the table. The waitress is coming with our food.

Children move back to the circle in the role of the customer again. The waitress (the teacher) gives out the orders, and the children eat their meal. Expect plenty of noise and conversation about the food. Allow this to happen, as long as the children remain seated and there is no pushing or yelling. Let the children explore and enjoy the improvisation. However, you may need to gently remind the children about the 'rules'.

WAITRESS: Did you enjoy your meal?

CHILDREN: Yes/no, it was _____.

TEACHER: Let's get our money out to pay the waitress.

WAITRESS: Thank you. That will be £2. Thank you for coming, please come again! Oh dear, we have so many dirty dishes to wash now. Can you help me?

Ask the children to stand and face a partner and hold both their hands. They chant 'wash the dishes, dry the dishes' as the swing their arms one way and then the other, then they chant 'turn the dishes over', as they try to turn around in a mirrored circle without letting go of their partner's hands. Repeat this several times.

Story

Sit the class in the audience position. Select a few children to play the following roles: waitress/waiter, customers, chef, manager.

Set up a simple restaurant by placing two or three chairs for the customers. Stand the chef (or chefs) behind another chair as their kitchen. You may wish to use a few simple props such as a wooden spoon, a bowl or a handbag. Keep it to minimum to ensure the children aren't distracted.

Narrate a simple story while the selected children improvise and 'act out' the story. Encourage the children to speak loudly and clearly, use mime, interact with one another and face out to the front. Allow the children to explore improvisation as you tell the story, but use the narration to keep the activity 'on track' and cohesive.

- *In a small street in a little village there was restaurant.*

- *There were some customers walking by who were very hungry.*

- *They stopped at the restaurant.*

- *They were greeted and welcomed inside by the manager. The customers were seated at a table.*

- *The waiter/waitress came and gave them a menu.*
- *The customers looked at the menu and decided what to order.*

The waiter or waitress takes the orders.

- *The waiter/waitress took the orders to the kitchen.*

The waitress/waiter repeats the orders to the chef.

- *The chef got busy cooking the food.*

The customers mime or improvise a conversation.

- *The chef announced that the food was ready.* (Use a bell.)
- *The waiter/waitress took the food to the customers.*
- *The customers ate their food.*

The customers comment on the food.

- *The customers paid the manager and left the restaurant.*
- *Well done, actors, stand tall and take a bow.*
- *Audience, can you give them a round of applause?*

Ask the actors to sit and join the audience and select different children to play the roles. Explain that you are going to do the story again, but this time you are going to add a 'problem' to make the story more interesting and entertaining for the audience. Brainstorm ideas for a problem – the food is bad, there's a fire in the kitchen, the chef adds too much chilli powder, the customers keep changing their minds, the waiter trips over and spills the food. Continue to rotate the actors and repeat with slightly different stories. You may also like to add more actors to the scene as the children become familiar with the story.

FINISH
Chef's Surprise

Divide the class into pairs. One is the chef and the other is the customer. Ask the chef to dish out lots of meals and snacks for the customer to taste that are either delicious or disgusting. For example: a bowl of spicy snakes, a giant chocolate cake, crunchy worms or five layers of jelly. The customer must mime eating the dishes using appropriate facial expressions and comments.

Extension

Divide the class into small groups and ask them to present their own scene in a restaurant. They must present a scene called 'Disaster at the Restaurant.' Use some of the ideas from above or let the children come up with their own ideas for a disaster.

Give each group 5–10 minutes to prepare before seating everyone in the audience position. Show each group's work, encouraging the actors to take a bow and the audience to applaud at the end of each scene.

Extracurricular Activities

Invite a local restaurateur to discuss their job with your class. Extend this further by inviting other people to come in and talk about their jobs.

- Create a 'dream menu' – talk about favourite foods.

- Bring in play money. Sort, identify and use for simple math activities.

- Make snack time into a pretend 'restaurant time'. The teacher in role as the waiter/waitress brings the children their food.

- Create an outdoor restaurant with real or pretend food.

- Create playdough food. Cut out shapes, roll sausages and squeeze out spaghetti.

- Cut out pictures of food from newspapers and magazines. Create a menu or a healthy food pyramid.

- Foods from home – invite families in to cook their favourite food or meals specific to their culture.

- Go to a local restaurant.

- Encourage children to try new foods.

- Visit a local produce market where children buy ingredients for a recipe.

Space

Resources

- Space music.
- A large piece of fabric.
- Some little star-shaped sequins.

WARM-UP
Space Walks

Ask the children to stand and find a space of their own. Remind the children that there is no running or touching anybody else. When the children are settled, use the following instructions:

- *Can you walk forward around the space? Freeze. Good freezes, everyone.*

- *As you move, can you find a bouncy way to move?*

- *Good, now can you walk sideways? Freeze.*

- *Can you find a light and gentle way to move? Excellent! Freeze.*

- *Now can you walk backwards? Freeze.*

- *Can you find a stiff and robotic way of moving? Good work! Freeze.*

- *Now let's try and walk fast with little steps. Freeze.*

- *Can you find a wobbly way to move? I like those wobbly walks. Freeze.*

- *Can you return to your natural walk?*

- *Now let's come and sit down.*

FOCUS
Teacher in Role

Tell the children they are going on a new adventure today, somewhere out of this world! They are going to take an adventure on board a rocket ship. You may wish to take on the role of a spaceship commander and ask the children to become your crew.

> COMMANDER: Okay, I'm going to need a crew of brave astronauts. We will soon be launching into space on a mission to explore the universe. Space crew, please put on your space suits. Next, you're going to need your big space boots. Please now put on your helmet. Mission control, do you read? We are ready for launch. I repeat, we are ready for launch.

Create the 'rocket' by forming a tight circle in the centre of the room and ask the children to raise their arms so their fingers are all connecting in the centre. Depending on the age group of your class, either count backwards from ten to one, or from five to one or, for very young children, count from one to five. At the end of counting, say together 'blast off'. Ask the children to 'fly through space' – moving as individuals around the room using a 'shhh' sound as they fly. After a few moments, ask the children to 'come in for landing' by slowing down, then lowering their arms as they chant 'beep, beep, beep... shhh.'

> COMMANDER: Okay crew. We have landed. Mission control, we have landed on what seems to be a planet made entirely of jelly. Astronauts, look around you. Everything is made of jelly. Let's open the doors and explore. Shall we taste some? How do we move around on planet jelly? Come on, let's go exploring.

Allow the children to play and explore moving around. Expect a lot of talk and discussion. You can always bring the control and focus back by assuming the role of the commander. After some time on Planet Jelly, ask the children to prepare for take-off.

Repeat the rocket-ship position, countdown, blast-off, flying and landing. Visit other planets using the children's suggestions for planet names. Ask them if there are any dangers on the planet, what things we will see, what sounds we might hear, what things we can eat. For example:

- *On Planet Zygor, beware of the bibble-babbles.*
- *Look over there – it's a snuggle tree. Listen to the sound it makes.*
- *Let's eat some Zygor soup.*
- *What else can we do here?*
- *How do we walk?*
- *How do we say 'hello'?*
- *Do we need our space helmets? Can we breathe the air?*

Slow Motion

After visiting a number of planets, return back towards school. Zoom past the planets you have visited, naming them as you go. Land on the Moon just before you return to earth.

> COMMANDER: Mission control – come in, we are now on the moon. We will return to earth soon, but first we are going to explore how we move on the Moon. Astronauts, there is less gravity here, so everything we do will happen in slow motion. Let's try to:
>
> o wave
> o walk
> o turn
> o fall
> o roll
> o eat
> o drink
> o run

Play the space music, and explore a few minutes of slow motion. Ask them to do these activities in slow motion. This will also allow the children's energy to calm down and to regain focus. Return to the rocket-ship position for the final time and return to Earth.

FINISH
Return to Earth

Return to Planet Earth. As the children come down for their final landing, ask them to lie down together on their backs. Hold the fabric over their heads (you will need an adult assistant, or select a child, to hold the other end) and gently lift and drop the fabric over the children, never letting it touch them. Insist that they remain as still as possible, with their legs and arms flat on the floor. Play the space music softly in the background, and use a gentle voice to remind the children about all the places they visited and what they saw. You may want to use the following as an example:

- *Have you ever looked up into the night sky and seen all the hundreds and thousands of stars up in the sky? Sometimes we can see the moon shining down on us. And some of those stars are the other planets in our solar system. And sometimes, if you are very, very lucky, you may even see a falling star. If ever you do, be sure to make a wish!*

Ask the children to close their eyes. Remove the fabric. Sprinkle little star-shaped sequins around the classroom. Ask the children to open their eyes and see if they can find a fallen star.

Extension

Visit planets from our solar system using information and statistics from the children's research. For example: visit Mercury and experience the intense heat, visit Jupiter and experience the biggest storm, or visit the dwarf planet Pluto and experience the icy core. You can create a physical model of the solar system by dividing the children into the different planets of our solar system. Be sure to include the Sun. Use extra children for the bigger planets and only one or two for the smaller planets. Bring it to life by asking the planets to remain in order whilst orbiting the centrally placed Sun. Build the exercise by adding music and instruments to create atmosphere or climax. Add narrative and use fabric for costumes.

Extracurricular Activities

- Read relevant books about space, rockets, space travel and aliens.

- Make some simple 2D planets by decorating paper circles. Arrange them on black construction paper to create a class mural.

- Use star- and circle-shaped cookie cutters with playdough.

- Sing 'Twinkle Twinkle Little Star'.

- Decorate small or large boxes to create rocket ships.

- Use the sandpit as the 'surface of a new planet', or as the Moon.

- Bring in glow-in-the-dark stars and create dark places to view them.

- Visit a planetarium.

- Discuss the phases of the Moon.

- Discuss how travelling to different countries can sometimes feel like a different planet – with their different languages, food, cultures and countryside, for instance.

- Make a string of stars by asking each child to make and decorate a star and attach them all on a string to hang in your room.

Under the Sea

Resources

- Several coloured scarves, or squares of material or mats.
- Warm-up music and relaxation music.
- A large shell.
- A long blue piece of fabric.
- Some little shells or star-shaped sequins.

WARM-UP
Moving Around the Space

Ask the children to stand and find their own space in the room. Remind the children that there is no running or touching anyone else. When the children are settled, use the following instructions:

- *Let's begin by walking around the space. As you are moving, I'm going to ask you to think about your steps. We are going to change our steps. Are you ready?*

- *Can you make your steps heavy?*

- *Good, now can you make them as light as you can?*

- *Fantastic work. Now make your steps very long. I like the way you aren't touching anybody else.*

- *Now let's make our steps very, very small.*

- *Good, can you make your steps fast? Remember, no running. Great work.*

- *Can you make your steps very slow? Well done, everyone, I like the way you were really thinking about changing your steps.*

- *Let's return to your natural walk.*

Musical Mats

Ask the children to sit along one side of the space. Lay some scarves around the space. Explain that these are going to be boats, and the rest of the floor is the ocean. Play some music and ask the children to move around as different animals from under the sea. When the music stops, the children must quickly move to one of the boats (or scarves). Ideas for creatures include:

- fish
- octopus
- jellyfish
- crab
- whale
- shark

The Edge of the Ocean

Ask the children to sit in a circle. Pass a large shell around the circle and ask the children to hold it to their ears and listen to the sound. After the children have listened to 'the ocean' in the shell, ask them to stand along one side of the space. Lay out the long blue fabric to represent the ocean. Hold one end and ask an assistant (or select one of the children) to hold the other end. Gently 'snake' the fabric back and forth along the ground. Ask the children to come down to the 'water's edge' without getting touched by the fabric. The children will move forwards and backwards together.

Into the Ocean

Hold the blue fabric at chest height. Again, you will need an assistant or another child to hold the other end. Invite the children under the fabric. Explain that they are now 'under the sea'. Ask the children to swim around. When the children are swimming, use the following instructions:

- *Check your goggles are on nice and tight.*

- *Good, now there's a lot to explore under the sea.*

- *What can you see?*

- *I can see some fish! Can you turn yourself into a fish? How might you use your hands to become fins? Good work, I like the way that you aren't touching anybody else.*

- *Can you return to your natural swimming?*

- *Okay, let's find out what else is hiding down here amongst the coral and rocks.*

- *I can see a clickety-clackety crab! Can you turn yourselves into a crab? Try to move sideways.*

Continue to explore different animals. Use the suggestions from the warm-up and the children's suggestions as well. As the children explore each animal, talk about the their size, colour, shape and movements. You may need to remove the fabric to ensure you have all the children engaged in the activity.

Dolphins

Ask the children to line up on one side of the room.
Hold the blue fabric at one end, with an assistant at
the other as if you are creating a wave. As you lift
the fabric up, select two or three children to 'swim'
under the 'wave' as if they are dolphins. When all
the children have reached the other side of the
wave, repeat the activity heading back to the other
side of the wave. Continue changing sides. It is
important to insist that the children do not go
under the fabric until it is their turn, otherwise
there may be collisions.

FOCUS
Story

Ask the children to sit in a circle. When they are settled, narrate the following introduction:

- *Today, we are going to create a story which is set under the sea.*

- *Can you think of some sea creatures that we have been exploring today which should be in our story?*

The children will name animals. If the children name animals that aren't found in the ocean, for example: frogs and elephants, help the children to identify where these animals would actually be found.

Encourage the children to think of a problem for the ocean story. You may like to ask questions such as: 'What would make the octopus sad?' or 'Why would the fish be frightened?'

Divide the children into small groups. Allocate each group a different sea creature. Set out different coloured pieces of material around the performance space and ask the children to sit on them. When the children are seated, narrate the story. You may wish to use the following as an example of a story:

- *Once upon a time, all the creatures of the sea were asleep.*

- *The fish were sleeping in the coral reef, the octopus in their cave, the jellyfish in their seaweed forest, the mermaids were sleeping in their castle and the crabs in their rock beds.*

- *One morning, the creatures woke up and stretched their fins and tentacles.*

- *The crabs were the first to wake up and they scurried out to find some food.*

Repeat the sequence of waking, searching for food, and returning 'home' with each group.

- *Just then, the fish had a good idea. It was the jellyfish's birthday, so they decided to organise an under-the-sea surprise party.*

Each group enters the central performance space and carries out their job for the party – food, presents, invitations, decorations and so forth.

- *When everything was ready, they all found a good hiding place.*
- *When the jellyfish arrived, the others all yelled out 'Surprise!' It was the most wonderful under-the-sea party anyone could remember.*

Encourage the children to dance, play, eat and drink.

- *When it was over, the jellyfish thanked everyone for the great party, and everyone waved goodbye to each other, and returned to their beds.*

The children return to their mats.

- *They fell asleep quickly, and all dreamt of the fabulous time they had.*

You might like to extend this further by adding a problem to the story. For example: the jellyfish group believe that everyone has forgotten their birthday, or the other creatures get lost on the way to the party.

FINISH

Ask the children to lie down under the blue fabric, holding it over them with an assistant (or one of the students) holding the other end. Play the relaxation music, and gently wave the fabric over the children. Put the fabric away, and ask the children to close their eyes and listen to the music. Sprinkle small stars or shells around the room. When the children open their eyes, ask them to see if they can find any shells or starfish on the beach.

Extension

Divide the class into groups and explore some other story ideas:

- The rubbish some people have left behind – an environmental focus.

- Find treasure under the ocean: where did it come from? What will we do with it?

- One of the characters gets lost and the others must work together to rescue them.

Extracurricular Activities

- Explore sea creatures. Use non-fiction books, posters, maps, etc.

- Discuss Planet Earth – use a globe or world map to identify the oceans. Discuss how most of the earth's surface is covered by water.

- Talk about activities we can do at the beach and in the ocean.

- Fill a big container with blue cellophane and cut out pictures of fish and other sea creatures. Attach a paper clip to each and make a fishing rod with a magnet attached.

- Make a starfish by decorating a paper cut-out of a star with sticker dots.

- Visit the beach, a marina or an aquarium.

- Eat fish and chips.

- Set up a small fish tank in your classroom.

Frogs

Resources

- A coloured scarf or square of fabric for each child.
- Appropriate music for warm-up.
- Diagrams and pictures about the life cycle of a frog (optional).
- 'Five Green and Speckled Frogs'.

WARM-UP
Moving Animals

Ask the children to find their own space in the room. When the children are focused, use the following instructions:

- *Animals move in many different ways. We are going to move like different animals.*
- *Can you gallop like a horse?*
- *Can you slither like a snake?*
- *Can you plod like a dinosaur?*
- *Can you scurry like a beetle?*
- *Can you jump like a rabbit?*
- *Can you think of another animal that jumps?*

  CHILDREN: A frog!

Discuss

Ask the children to sit in a circle and discuss what they know about frogs. Questions you may like to ask include:

- *Where do frogs live?*
- *What colours are frogs?*
- *What sound do they make?*
- *What do they eat?*
- *What else do you know about frogs?*

After discussing what the children know about frogs, ask them to show you how a frog moves.

Lily Pads

Ask the children to sit on one side of the space. Spread some of the scarves around the space and explain to the children that they are lily pads. The rest of the space is the pond. Ask the children to move around the space, swimming in the pond and resting on the lily pads. Play some music. When the music stops, the children must jump on to a lily pad.

Growing into Frogs

Ask the children to find their own space in the room. When the children are settled, ask them to crouch down and imagine they are in an 'egg'. Cover each child with a scarf. When the children hatch out of their eggs, collect the scarves until the end of the story.

- *Once upon a time, there was a tiny egg, waiting in the pond.*
- *One night, when the moon was high in the sky, the little egg popped and out came a little tadpole.*
- *The little tadpole swam around the pond, wiggling its long tail.*
- *Then one day, the tadpole did something amazing. It grew two back legs.*
- *The tadpole got bigger and bigger, and one day, it grew two front legs.*
- *The tadpole looked at itself and wondered.*
- *Then as it was swimming around, it noticed that its tail was getting smaller and smaller, until finally it was gone!*
- *The tadpole realised it wasn't a tadpole any more.*
- *It was a frog.*
- *The frog liked to jump onto the lily pads and say hello to all the other frogs.*

As you narrate the end of the story, spread out the scarves as lily pads again. Finish with the frogs sitting on their own lily pad.

Discuss

Ask the children to sit on the lily pads and discuss the life cycle of a frog. You may want to use diagrams and pictures. The children may already know about the life cycle of a frog, but ask them open-ended questions. Try and cover the facts that frogs lay eggs, the eggs hatch into tadpoles, they grow back legs, front legs, lose their tail and learn to come out of the water.

FOCUS
Five Green and Speckled Frogs

Ask the children to sit on the audience mat. Teach the children the song 'Five Green and Speckled Frogs' (you can find it online if you don't know it already). Sit the class in audience position. Choose five children at a time to enter the performance space as the speckled frogs. Sing the song together as the three children perform the song in mime and movement. Repeat until most of the children have had a turn.

- *I once saw five little green and speckled frogs, and would you believe they were all sitting on a speckled log!*

- *Let's sing the song!*

On the first line, the children should sit in 'frog' position on the log (the scarf). On the second line, the children should mime eating. On the third, the children should say 'yum yum!' And on the final line, one of the children should hop offstage. Repeat until there are no frogs left.

You can also select a bigger group to perform and select more children to jump into the pool at one time.

FINISH
Froggy Froggy

Ask the children to sit in a circle. Ask one child to sit in the centre as the frog, crouched down and eyes closed. Place a 'bug' (either use a plastic toy or any small object) behind the child in the centre. The rest of the class chant 'Froggy, Froggy, who's got your bug?' Select one child to get the bug and hide it behind their back. Ask everyone else to put their hands behind their backs as well and have a 'guilty' or 'sneaky' face. The children chant 'Wake up, Froggy, who's got your bug?' The frog opens their eyes and has three guesses as to who has the bug.

Divide the class into pairs and ask them to practise 'leapfrog'. Child A is crouched down low on the ground. Child B places their hands on A's shoulders and leaps over them. Swap roles.

Extend the activity by getting long lines of children to crouch down as other children leapfrog over them.

Extension

Divide the class into small groups and ask them to present a small scene about a 'frog story'. Ideas include the frog who lost his croak, the frog who wanted to be a duck, how the frog got his croak, the tadpoles go on an adventure in the pond, the frog meets the toad. Ask the children to include the role of a narrator.

Extracurricular Activities

- Read stories about frogs.
- Make 'frog in a pond' – set a chocolate frog in green jelly.
- Make a frog paper-plate puppet. Colour a paper plate and attach two ping-pong balls on the top for eyes. Draw in some eyeballs on the balls. Draw two small dots for nostrils and a big red mouth. Attach a straw or lolly stick at the back. Have a frog puppet show with your friends.

- Have a green day – wear green, eat green food and drink green drinks, decorate your room in green, make green artwork.

- Make three speckled frogs by decorating three separate cups from an egg carton and then make a log by painting one line of the egg carton.

- Draw a huge lily pad or cut one out from construction paper. Ask all the children to draw a frog, cut it out and paste on the lily pad.

- Visit the zoo.

- Find out what other animals and insects undergo metamorphosis.

- Talk about the environmental impact on frog habitats.

- Discuss which parts of the country or the world frogs come from.

- Talk about the difference between the smallest and largest frogs of the world.

Bugs and Beetles

Resources

- Several large pieces of fabric.

WARM-UP
Waking Up Our Bodies

Ask the children to stand in a circle. Remind the children not to run or touch anybody else. When the children are settled, use the following instructions:

• *Let's begin by raising our shoulders up to our ears. Good, and down.*

Repeat.

• *Let's roll our shoulders around. And now roll them the other way.*

• *Take a big breath in and raise your arms up. Now, as you breathe out, move your hands down to your toes.*

• *Let's do that again, take a big breath in and reach up. And breathe out and reach down to your toes.*

• *Now let's change our whole bodies. Can you make your body very big? Good and now make your whole body small.*

• *Can you make your body:*

  o *flat?*
  o *wide?*
  o *soft?*
  o *spiky?*
  o *fast?*
  o *slow?*

Continue the activity and increase the difficulty level by asking the children to show you combinations of shapes and speed such as the examples below.

• *Now let's move around the space.*

• *I'm going to see if you can move your body in many different ways.*

• *You need to listen to my instructions. Ready?*

• *Can you make your movements:*

  o *big and slow?*
  o *spiky and fast?*
  o *wide and slow?*
  o *flat and fast?*
  o *soft and slow?*
  o *small and fast?*

Allow the children a few moments to explore each new way of moving.

Build the exercise by repeating these different ways of moving with a partner or in a small group.

For older children, challenge them to move as a whole group together.

Imaginary Insects

- *Imagine your hands are tiny little insects crawling from your toes up to your chin, and now on to your heads.*

- *Let them crawl over your face and onto your shoulders.*

- *Now let them creep down your chest and around behind your back.*

Discuss

Ask the children to sit in a circle. Discuss what they know about bugs and insects. Questions you may like to ask the children include:

- *Can you name any bugs, beetles and insects?*

- *What do you know about insects?*

As the children name insects, spend a short time exploring the movement of each one. Try to identify their characteristics with the children. Is it fast or slow? Flat or wide? Spiky or soft? Does it fly or crawl?

Bugs, beetles and insects that you may want to explore include ants, centipedes, ladybirds, beetles, grasshoppers, mosquitoes, flies, honey bees and caterpillars.

FOCUS
Our Insect Story

Ask the children to sit in a circle. When they are settled, use the following instructions:

- *We are now going to create a story set inside the world of insects.*
- *What kinds of insects should be in our story?*

Create a list of three to five different insects.

- *What can our story be about?*
- *Remember, if we want our story to be even more interesting, we need a problem.*

Continue to brainstorm with the children a story about all the insects working together to solve a problem. There could be a large object which they need to carry or move, they may need to find food, build a new home or nest, avoid the anteater or cross a river. The important message is that cooperation is the key to solving the problem. Be sure to keep the story simple. Once the storyline is agreed, divide the class into groups of insects. Sit each group on a large piece of fabric to help define the space. You may need to select some children to be the audience. Let them know they will swap later. Narrate the story whilst the children act it out in the centre. Allow opportunities for the children to say lines and to explore dialogue between characters. Look for opportunities for chorus work, when the children say the same thing at the same time, for example: 'Everybody pull together!' or 'How will we cross the river?'

FINISH

Play the game 'Imaginary Insects' again (page 199), but this time ask the children to make the creeping, crawling, buzzing, chirping insect sounds.

Extension

Divide the class into small groups and give them time to improvise a scene set in the insect world. You may need to give them a title for their improvisation, for example 'how the bee got its stripes', 'the day the ants found the feast' or 'why the caterpillar needs so many legs'. Encourage more dialogue between the characters. Give each group 5–10 minutes to prepare and practise and remind the children to use loud clear voices and face the front when they present their work to an audience.

Extracurricular Activities

- Make caterpillars by threading beads onto a pipe-cleaner, or by gluing pompoms together.

- Take magnifying glasses outside and try to find some insects.

- Make 'ants on a log' by spreading cream cheese or similar on a carrot or celery stick and sticking on sultanas for the ants.

- Read relevant books, both fiction and non-fiction.

- Make some bugs – you can use playdough, clay, straws, pipe-cleaners or beads, for instance.

- Do some finger-painting – when dry add details such as legs, wings or eyes with a black felt tip pen.

- Discuss bugs around the world. Look for good documentaries.

- Find out which insects are venomous or dangerous.

- Make some antennae using headbands and pipe-cleaners.

- Research honey bees and honey production.

Spiders

Resources

- 'Incy Wincy Spider'.
- 'Little Miss Muffet'.
- A large piece of fabric.
- Chairs or scarves for half the class.

WARM-UP
Open, Shut Them

Ask the children to sit in a circle. Once the children have settled, use the following instructions:

- *Let's begin by shaking our hands. Can you shake them even faster?*
- *Good, now let's stretch our hands out wide. How wide can you stretch your hands?*
- *Good, now can you close them all up?*
- *Good, now open them out wide again.*
- *And shut them tight.*
- *Excellent work.*
- *Let's imagine that our hands are two big, creepy spiders.*
- *Show me your creeping hands again. Can you creep them along the floor in front of you?*
- *Good, now creep them back on to your lap.*
- *Can you creep your hands up your tummy to your shoulders?*
- *And now creep them on to your face and on to the top of your head.*
- *Show me your scared face.*
- *Creep them back down to your shoulders, down the front of your body and on to your lap.*
- *Let's make them creep along the waterspout.*

Incy Wincy Spider

Sing the song 'Incy Wincy Spider' with the children. Once the children are familiar with the words, ask the children to stand up and imagine they are 'incy wincy'. Encourage lots of actions and miming.

Discuss

Ask the children to sit in a circle. When the children are settled, discuss what they know about spiders. You may like to ask questions such as:

- *Are you scared of spiders?*
- *What do they eat?*
- *Where have you seen a spider?*
- *How many legs do spiders have?*
- *Some are very big, some are small and some are poisonous!*

FOCUS
Spinning Webs

Discuss how spiders spin webs and why (to catch food, attract other spiders, build a home). Ask the children to find a space of their own in the room. When the children are settled, ask them to take on a small position. Narrate the following:

* *Imagine you are a tiny little spider.*
* *The sun has gone to bed, and the moon is high in the night sky.*
* *Wake up, little spiders, it's time to spin your web.*
* *You will need to start by making a web from one side to the other. And now can you make a web across the other way?*
* *Join the lines together, moving around and around.*
* *It's finished.*
* *And now, little spider, rest right in the middle of your beautiful web. Wait... wait... wait... as still as you can.*
* *You can hear something buzzing. A fly!*
* *It has landed onto your sticky web and is making the web wiggle.*
* *Slowly creep out towards the fly and... catch it!*
* *Wrap it up in some of your sticky web and save it there for later.*

Silent Scream

Ask the children to find their own space in the room. When the children are settled, use the following instructions:

* *What sound do we make when we are frightened?*
* *That's right, we yell or scream.*
* *We are going to scream without making any noise.*
* *Can you show me a silent scream?*
* *It's just like a real scream but there is NO NOISE, we just use our faces.*

- *Let's try it.*
- *Very good silent screams, everyone.*
- *Let's try it again!*

Discuss

Ask the children to sit together on the fabric. Ask them if they know another nursery rhyme with a spider. The children may have many different answers. You might like to ask the children if they know the nursery rhyme where a spider frightens a little girl called Little Miss Muffet.

Little Miss Muffet

Teach the children the song 'Little Miss Muffet'. Sing through the song and ask the children to nominate one of their hands as 'Miss Muffet' and the other hand as the 'spider'. Repeat the song and encourage the children to find a way to use their hands and fingers whilst they are singing the song.

Divide the class into two groups. One group will become the spiders and the other will become Miss Muffets. (If your group is large, you may want to nominate a third group to be the audience.) Sit the spiders on a large piece of fabric, which is the 'giant web'. Sit the other group on chairs or scarves as their tuffets. (If you have a third group, sit them in the audience position.) Sing the song again, but this time, ask the children to act it out. You may also invite the children to say a line. Remind the children to face their audience and to speak loudly and clearly.

Swap the roles of the groups and repeat. Ensure that the children have a turn at each role (and as the audience, if you have three groups).

FINISH

Ask the children to find a space of their own. The children can either stand or sit, as long as they are in a comfortable position. When the children are settled, use the following instructions:

- *Let's imagine that we are spiders waiting on our silvery spider webs.*

- *Show me your long spidery legs. Can you stretch them out, one by one?*

- *And now, let's wrap ourselves up in our own web and fall asleep.*

- *All the spiders are asleep on their webs after a very busy day.*

- *Let's take a big breath in and as you breathe out, relax all your legs and your whole body.*

- *Now, as we breathe in, wake up and stretch all your legs.*

- *Can you stand up and take a spidery bow? Give yourselves a spidery clap.*

Extension

Build the performance by adding props (such as bowls or spoons) and simple costumes. Ask the children to improvise a few lines of dialogue between Miss Muffet and the spider.

For older children, give them a scriptwriting task. Ask them to complete a different rhyme which begins with either 'Little Miss Muffet' or 'Incy Wincy Spider'.

Divide the children into groups (or partners) and ask them to improvise a scene called, 'How Miss Muffet and Incy Wincy Became Friends'.

Extracurricular Activities

- Create edible spiders – cake body, chocolate-finger legs and eight sultana eyes.

- Make some spiders from playdough using pipe-cleaner for their legs.

- Make some paper spiders – use a circle for the body with eight paper legs in concertina fold or paper curl.
- Create a spider web – give the children a ball of string or ribbon and ask them to thread, tie and weave a small web.
- Read and discuss non-fiction books about spiders and other insects from around the world.
- Explore outdoors in search of spiders and other insects with a magnifying glass.
- Give the children a ball of wool or string and ask them to tie up the whole classroom in a giant spider web.
- Discuss poisonous and dangerous spiders from around the world.
- Watch online videos of spiders in action.
- Discuss arachnophobia and other fears and phobias.
- Buy fake spiders and hide them around your classroom!

Transport

Resources

- Chairs or scarves.
- A hat or simple costume piece for teacher in role (optional).
- 'The Wheels on the Bus'.
- Relaxation music.
- A long piece of fabric.

WARM-UP
Along the Line

Create a straight line on the floor by using chalk, string, rope or a length of fabric. Identify the start and finish of the line. Ask the children to line up at the starting point. When the children are settled use the following instructions:

- *Can you walk along the line?*

- *Good, now we are going to move along the path in different ways.*

- *Can you:*
  - *creep?*
  - *crawl?*
  - *roll?*
  - *skip?*
  - *hop?*
  - *limp?*
  - *march?*
  - *spin?*
  - *move quickly?*
  - *move slowly?*
  - *walk stiffly?*
  - *walk in a wobbly way?*
  - *take light steps?*
  - *take heavy steps?*

Playing with Transportation

Ask the children to line up at the start of the line again. When the children are settled, use the following instructions with the children:

- *Let's imagine that the line on our floor is a road.*

- *Now let's pretend to move along the path as if we are driving a big truck. How big is the steering wheel? What sound does your truck make? Do you know what a truck horn sounds like?*

- *Good. Now let's move along our road in a car. Can you beep the horn?*

- *Let's get on our motorbike now. Put on your helmet and big boots. How do we hold on to the handlebars?*

- *Now let's go along a bumpy road on a slow tractor. What sound does a tractor make?*

- *What about a boat, how we can pretend to move along the water in a boat?*

- *Now let's imagine our road has become a runway. Prepare to take off in an aeroplane. How can we show that we are in a plane?*

- *And lastly, let's imagine our runway is a railway track. Let's all join together to make a train.*

Discuss

Ask the children to sit in a circle. When the children are settled, ask them how they got to class that day. It's probable that many children arrived in a car. Continue the discussion on transportation. You may like to ask the children:

- *What other types of transport can you think of? Make a list of different forms of transport.*

FOCUS
A Transportation Journey

Ask the children to find their own space in the room. When the children are settled, use the following instructions:

• *Today, we are going to go on a long journey.*

• *We will be using lots of different kinds of transport. But we are going to begin our journey by train.*

• *Let's go!*

Build a train by placing chairs in a line in rows of two. If there are no chairs, use scarves or a long piece of fabric.

• *Let's go and get our tickets!*

Teacher in Role

The teacher plays the roles of the ticket seller, stationmaster and train driver. You may want to use a hat or another simple costume piece to help you get into each role. Try to use a different voice from your own, maybe a deeper voice or use an accent. This will ensure that you can switch easily between roles.

> TICKET SELLER: Everyone line up. Please purchase a ticket. Once you have a ticket, please find a seat on the train. Don't forget to leave the front seat for the driver.

> STATIONMASTER: All aboard. The train to the beach is departing from platform seven in one minute. All passengers must have a valid ticket! Please remain seated at all times. All aboard!

Blow the train's 'whistle'.

> TRAIN DRIVER: All aboard!

Sit at the front of the train. Children can make choo-choo sounds and rotate their arms as though they are the wheels as the train 'moves'. Go up hills (slow movement and sound), down hills (fast movement and sound), around corners (children lean out to one side), through dark tunnels, blow the whistle. Arrive at the station.

- *We have now arrived at the last station.*
- *It's a very long walk to the beach from the station.*
- *Let's catch that bus!*

Transport Story

Keep the chairs in the same arrangement. Ask the children to imagine that the chairs now represent the bus. Sit the children in the chairs. Sing a few versus of 'The Wheels on the Bus'.

After singing the song, use the following script to advance the story.

- *Oh dear, the bus is making some very weird noises.*
- *I think this bus has a problem with the engine.*
- *But it's still a long way to the beach.*
- *How are we going to get there now?*
- *Can you see another form of transport nearby?*

Allow the children to find a solution. Perhaps they spot some motorbikes for hire, a horse and cart or some scooters. After a few moments on the next transport, identify another problem – for example: the motorbikes might run out of petrol. Continue on your journey to the beach, exploring different modes of transport using the children's suggestions. Explore many different ideas. Use rollerskates and have the wheels fall off. Walk and get tired feet.

Eventually arrive at the beach. While there, you may continue to explore various types of water transport. Go on a speedboat, a gentle yacht ride or row a boat. Exhausted, you may want to call your private jet or helicopter to fly you back to school.

FINISH
Relaxation

Play some relaxation music. Ask the children to lie on their backs. Stretch out a long piece of fabric over their heads at waist height (you will need someone to hold the other end). Use a calm and soft voice to remind the children about all the different kinds of transport they used today. Allow the children some time to rest and then place the fabric on the floor. Sit the children on the fabric, or in a circle and ask them to think about their favourite kind of transport.

Musical Chairs

Arrange some chairs either in a circle, or in two rows, with the backs of the chairs together. Play some music and ask the children to move as a different mode of transport while the music is playing. When the music stops, the children must sit on a chair. Either play as elimination, or ask the children to sit on another person's lap as the chairs are taken away (for more detail on this, see page 231).

Extension

Divide the class into groups of 3–5 children. Ask each group to improvise a short scene about a trip that uses at least three different modes of transport. Each mode of transport must experience some kind of problem or breakdown. The scene must end with them arriving at their destination. Give the children 5–10 minutes to prepare and practise. Sit the class in audience position and show each group one at at time.

Extracurricular Activities

• Discuss modes of transport in other countries around the world.

• Make a class-sized train by attaching cardboard boxes together and decorate it.

- Visit a traffic school.

- Create a transport mural. Paint roads, tracks, sky and water on to a large sheet of paper. Use pictures from magazines or draw pictures and stick them onto the mural.

- Design your 'dream car' – invent a vehicle of the future.

- Set up a train track in class.

- Make paper boats.

- Have a 'bring your wheels to class day' – for instance, skateboards, trikes, bikes, toy trains or toy cars.

- Arrange an excursion using at least two different modes of transportation.

- Bring in a train, plane or bus timetable and discuss how to read them.

- Look for stories and picture books about different modes of transport.

- Look at a city map and highlight the roads, train tracks, tram tracks, rivers and any other transport lines.

- Explore sustainability and pollution from motor vehicles.

- Have a 'walk to school' day.

FOUR

WORKING WITH TEXTS

Going on a Bear Hunt

Resources

- A long piece of fabric.
- Michael Rosen's *We're Going on a Bear Hunt*.
- Relaxation music.

WARM-UP
A Walk in the Forest

Ask the children to move around the space. Remind them that there is no running or touching anybody else. When the children are settled, use the following instructions:

- *Let's begin by taking big steps. Good, now back to your natural walk.*
- *Let's take little steps. Good, now back to your natural walk.*
- *As you are moving, let's imagine that the ground below you is starting to change.*
- *How might you walk on hot sand? Good use of your imaginations. I like the way you are using your faces as well.*
- *Let's all imagine the ground is getting much cooler. The ground is now very cool and wet.*
- *Show me how you would walk through sticky mud. Very good, now let's move out of the mud.*
- *The ground is changing again. The whole room is changing.*
- *Can you imagine it is getting very dark? How do you walk in a dark forest? Good, I like the way you are slowing down.*
- *Now it's getting cold again. The ground is getting wet. There's lots of water. Now show me how it looks walking through a cold river. Excellent work, everyone!*
- *Can you return to your natural walk?*

Exploring with Fabric

Use the long piece of fabric. Stretch out the fabric with the children's help. Ask the children to stand along the edge of the fabric and hold on to the edges. When the children are settled, use the following instructions:

- *We are going to move in different ways with the fabric.*

- *Can we make it move fast?*
- *Can we make it move slowly?*
- *Hold on very tight.*
- *Can we make it go high?*
- *Good, can we make it go low?*
- *Good, now let's all sit on the fabric.*
- *Good, now let's all move off the fabric.*
- *Can you stand and move over the fabric?*
- *Can we find a way to go under the fabric?*
- *Let's all walk around the fabric.*

You will need an assistant, or select one of the children, to help you hold the other end.

- *When we lift up the fabric, can you go under it?*
- *Good, now we will bring the fabric down. Can you sit on it?*

Reading

If time permits, ask the children to remain seated and read the story *We're Going on a Bear Hunt*.

Mirrors

Stand or sit in front of the children who are sitting on the fabric. Ask them to mirror (copy) your moves. Start with simple movements and gradually increase their difficulty. For example: start with one hand, one arm, then two arms, then add in facial expressions. You may also wish to introduce some lines from the book and ask the children to say them back to you.

FOCUS
A Bear Hunt Story

Ask the students to sit on the ground in front of you. When they are settled, use the following instructions:

- *We are going on an adventure today.*
- *We are going on a hunt! Do you know what we are hunting?*
- *A... BEAR!*
- *We are going on a bear hunt!*
- *Let's imagine the bear hunt together.*

Ask the children to stand up and get ready to go on a bear hunt.

- *Let's get started by opening the gate.*

Read the story to the children and encourage them to make a gesture or sound after each line in the story. For example: the children may march on the spot to show they are going on a bear hunt or make the sound 'squelch, squelch, squelch' as they mime moving through the mud.

FINISH

After the children have completed the 'hunt' and 'returned to the room', ask the children to lie down under the fabric (you may need an assistant or ask a couple of children to help you). Gently lift the fabric up and down over the children while you play the relaxation music. As the children settle you may like to use the following instructions:

- *It's fun to go on an adventure.*
- *The bear hunt was very exciting.*
- *Now it's time to lie down and relax.*
- *You might like to close your eyes and remember the places we visited today.*

Game

Play 'King's Treasure' (page 37), but replace the king with the bear. The children creep up towards the bear and freeze as if they are parts of the forest whenever the bear turns around. When the children get close to the bear, the bear turns around and chases the children back to the start.

Extension

Divide the class into small groups. Allocate each group a different section of the book. Ask the children to rehearse their section of the book with greater detail than they used in the focus activity. Encourage improvised conversation and additional characterisation. For example: the children may become eerie creatures in the forest, fish in the river or bats in the cave.

Extracurricular Activities

- Draw or paint your favourite part of the bear hunt.
- Build a cave – indoors or outdoors. Use boxes, blankets, tables, fabric, etc.

- Play hide-and-seek where the seeker pretends to be a bear.
- Have a treasure hunt – indoors or outdoors. Hide simple objects such as beads, coloured balls, straws or bottle tops.
- Make mud pies.
- Make footprint paintings.
- Write or tell stories about your own bear hunt.
- Bring in different elements and materials for the children to explore with bare feet, for example: sand, cold water, grass, mud, clay or bubble wrap.

Goldilocks and the Three Bears

Resources

- A long piece of fabric.
- *Goldilocks and the Three Bears*.
- Chairs for musical chairs.

WARM-UP
Warm-up Circle

Begin with the 'Warm-up Circle' (see *Let's Get Started!*, page 2).

Playing with Voice

Ask the children to sit in a circle. When the children are settled, use the following instructions:

- *Let's all begin by saying 'good morning/afternoon'.*
- *Now let's say it again, but this time make your voice:*
  - *quiet*
  - *loud*
  - *grumpy*
  - *kind*
  - *like a baby*
  - *like you are very old*
  - *scared*
  - *excited*
- *Well done, everyone. We can change our voices in many different ways.*
- *In drama, we change our voices to show different emotions or feelings.*
- *We can also change our voices to help us become a different character.*

Playing with Character

Ask the children to find their own place in the room. When they are settled, use the following instructions:

- *Let's warm up the rest of our bodies now.*
- *Can you start by walking around the room in your natural walk? Excellent work, everyone.*
- *I want you to use your face and your bodies to show me different emotions and characters. As you are walking around, can you show me:*

- a quiet character
- a loud character
- a grumpy character
- a kind character
- a baby character
- a very old character
- a scared character
- an excited character

- *Well done, everyone. Let's return to our natural walk.*

Reading

If time permits, sit the children on the long fabric and read a version of *Goldilocks and the Three Bears*. As you read the children the story, encourage vocal participation (repeating some of the lines of the characters), facial expressions and use of gesture. The children should remain seated as you read the story.

FOCUS
Goldilocks and the Three Bears

Ask the children to find their own space in the room. When the children are settled use the following instructions:

- *Can you tell me the characters from this story?*

The children should call out the characters from *Goldilocks and the Three Bears*.

- *Well done, everyone! We are going to become each of these characters.*
- *As I call out one of the characters, can you show me how you would use your bodies and your faces?*

Explore each of the characters listed below. As the children move around the space, suggest how they might change their bodies and faces and give them a line from the story to repeat using a different voice.

PAPA BEAR – big, tall, round belly, strong shoulders, big loud voice.

MAMA BEAR – busy with household chores, quick steps, kind face, polite.

BABY BEAR – small steps, baby voice, curious, playful, little paws.

GOLDILOCKS – skipping with basket, happy, long curly hair, hungry tummy.

After exploring each of the characters, narrate the story and ask the children to mime the characters and their actions and repeat the lines.

After going through the story as a whole class, ask the children to sit in the audience position and select four children to play the roles of the three bears and Goldilocks. Encourage performers them to face the audience, use a big speaking voice and change their bodies to show character. Remind the audience to give a round of applause. Repeat a short version of the story until all the children have had a turn performing. You may need to group the children into characters, for example: three children play the role of each character and perform together. Do not force any child to perform. All the children should be good audience members, though, regardless of their participation as performers.

FINISH

Play musical chairs, encouraging the children to dance or move as one of the characters from the story. Before you start playing the game, remind the children of the safety rules. To play the game, place two rows of chairs back to back in the centre of the room. Play some music and when the music stops, the children must quickly find a chair to sit on. Remove a chair after each round. You can play the game as an elimination or non-elimination version. For the elimination version: the child who does not get a seat is eliminated. In the non-elimination version, the child must sit on another person's lap if they can't find a chair. There may be 4–5 children sitting on each other's laps. In either version, continue to remove a chair after each round, until there are only a few chairs left.

Sit the children on a mat and place a chair in front of the group. Select a child to sit on the chair, blindfolded. Select another child to stand behind the seated child and say 'hello'. The child on the chair must try and identify the class member by listening to the voice. Make the game harder by asking the child to use a 'different' voice when they say 'hello'.

Extension

Divide the story into separate lines and give each child a line to learn. Repeat the story using the children as narrators, the forest, house and furniture. You can develop the activity further by choosing some children to play instruments to accompany the action or by using scarves as the set (chairs, table cloth, beds and so forth). Develop this into a performance and invite a real audience to watch.

Extracurricular Activities

• Make a teddy bear mask from a paper plate.

• Make a Goldilocks headband by stapling a fringe made of card and attaching strips of newspaper or coloured paper for curls.

- Make and eat some porridge.
- Make some 'beds' that are too hard (use wood or plastic), too soft (lots of cushions and blankets) and just right (ask the children for ideas to make the 'ideal bed').
- Draw or paint your favourite character from the story.
- Write your own story about going to the house of the three bears.
- Create a sculpture of a bear using clay or playdough.
- Discuss fractured fairytales and twisted endings. Encourage the children to create a different story based on *Goldilocks and the Three Bears*.
- Take a walk in the woods, or turn your classroom into the woods using fabric and natural materials.

Nursery Rhymes 1

Resources

- 'Humpty Dumpty'.
- 'Jack and Jill'.
- A long piece of fabric.

WARM-UP
Exploring Humpty Dumpty

Ask the children to sit in a circle. When the children are settled, sing the nursery rhyme 'Humpty Dumpty'. Sing through the song with the children and encourage them to explore different ways of presenting the song using their fingers and hands as Humpty and the wall.

Humpty Dumpty Character

Ask the children to find their own space in the room. Remind the children that during the activity they should not touch anyone else or make a sound. When the children are settled, use the following instructions:

- *Let's walk around the space using our natural walk.*

- *As you are walking, imagine you are getting bigger and bigger.*

- *As you get bigger and bigger show how:*
  - o *your tummy is getting rounder*
  - o *your chest is getting fuller*
  - o *you are so big and round that your walk becomes a waddle*
  - o *your body is like a big round egg.*

- *Wow, you are a big Humpty Dumpty.*

- *Our legs are tired from all that walking. Let's try to sit down.*

- *Here is a good spot to sit. On this wall!*

The children sit.

- *Uh-oh! We are a bit too big for this wall.*

- *The wall is starting to wobble! Oh no!*

The children fall.

- *We've had a great fall!*

Discuss

When the children are settled, discuss their experiences of accident and injury. Questions you may like to ask include:

- *Have you ever broken any bones?*
- *Have you had a bad fall?*
- *Have you ever been very sick?*
- *It is important that we remember to look after ourselves when we are sick or hurt.*
- *Who else can look after you if you get sick?*

FOCUS
All the King's Horses

During this activity the teacher plays the role of captain of the king's men. When the children are reading, act out the scene as the king's men. As captain, you may like to give the following instructions to the students using a posh accent:

- *Stand tall.*

- *Attention, all royal men and royal horses.*

- *Please line up in front of your captain.*

- *A terrible thing has just happened. Humpty Dumpty has just fallen off the wall!*

Allow the children to react in character.

- *I need you to ride out to the wall and try to put him back together again.*

- *Come on, men, let's get on our royal horses and gallop to the wall. Giddy-up!*

Remain in role and mime getting on your horse. Encourage the children to do the same. Circle the space a few times with the children on 'horseback'. Be sure to keep the children safe by asking them to move in the same direction. Allow them to explore riding their 'horse', by using sound (neighing) or giving the horse instructions ('giddy-up', 'whoa, horse', 'faster, boy'). Also encourage them to steer their horse and to use the different paces such as trotting and galloping.

Rein your horses in as you begin to 'find' Humpty Dumpty.

The following dialogue is an example of what you may expect from a class of 3–5-year-olds.

> CAPTAIN: Oh dear. I have found a piece of Humpty Dumpty.

> CHILDREN: Here's one. I've found another one. Look, here are a whole lot of pieces!

> CAPTAIN: It's just like a big jigsaw puzzle. Can we try to put it back together?

> CHILDREN: I know! This piece goes here. And this piece goes there.

CAPTAIN: Well done, men. But how are we going to stick the pieces back together?

CHILDREN: Sticky tape. Glue. Rope. Magic.

CAPTAIN: Great ideas, king's men. Let's try all of those things. Humpty needs all the help he can get.

Let the children begin 'reconstructing' Humpty.

CAPTAIN: Oh dear, king's men. It looks like all the king's horses and all the king's men, can't put Humpty back together again. What a shame!

It is very likely that the children will desperately want to put Humpty back together which can become quite chaotic. Remain in the role as the captain and brainstorm as a group the best way/s to tackle the problem.

You can extend and deepen the drama by creating suspense. One way you may like to do this is to use the following instructions:

- *Let's build Humpty back up slowly. We want to make sure we put him back together correctly. Let's go through each 'body part' until he is finished.*

- *Are you ready? Help me to rebuild Humpy's:*
  o *feet*
  o *legs*
  o *body*
  o *arms*
  o *hand*
  o *face*
  o *hat*

Ask questions as you engage in this activity to create a sense of 'make-believe':

- *Where does this piece go?*
- *Who knows what this piece is?*
- *Where does this little hand go?*

When Humpty is finally finished, celebrate together. Join hands and dance around the imaginary Humpty.

CAPTAIN: Well done, men! What a great job. Let's get back on our horses and return to the castle to tell the king. Giddy-up!

Circle the space in the opposite direction from before.

Testing Humpty Dumpty

Ask the children to find their own space in the room. When the children are settled, use the following instructions:

- *Let's imagine that we are Humpty Dumpty, who has just been put back together again.*
- *Can we walk around the room as Humpty Dumpty? We have to walk very slowly and carefully.*
- *Can you show me how Humpty moves now? Very good, I like the way you are being very careful!*
- *He has had a very big fall, and needs to look after himself now.*
- *Let's go carefully to our Humpty Dumpty bed, and gently lie down, careful not to crack!*
- *And rest here in your bed. You've had a very big day!*

You may choose to finish the class here, go to the extension activities or continue if time permits.

- *I know another nursery rhyme where somebody has an accident, can you guess?*

Jack and Jill

Sing through the nursery rhyme 'Jack and Jill' with the children. After singing the nursery rhyme, discuss the terms: 'pail' (bucket), 'fetch' (get) and 'crown' (head).

Ask the children to find their own space in the room. When the children are settled, use the following instructions:

- *Let's all pretend that we are either Jack or Jill.*
- *Let's get our pail.*
- *Come on, let's all move over here so we can walk up this big hill.*

Move to one side of the room.

- *Oh dear, Jack, watch your step or you'll...*

Ask all the Jacks to roll down to the hill, to the other side of the room.

- *Oh no, Jill, look out!*

Ask all the Jills to roll down the hill towards to the other side of the room.

Alternatively, you may pair the children up and ask them to act out the nursery rhyme while the rest of the class sits in the audience position singing the song. Use a long piece of fabric for the hill. Encourage good miming and facial expressions. You may also want to use the second verse of the nursery rhyme. Remind the children to applaud after each group has performed.

FINISH

Play 'Duck, Duck, Goose', but use 'Humpty, Humpty, Dumpty' or 'Jack, Jack, Jill'.

Extension

Divide the class into small groups and ask them to recreate the nursery rhyme of 'Humpty Dumpty' or 'Jack and Jill' with a twisted ending. For older children, ask them to create their narrative in rhyme. Give each group 5–10 minutes to plan and practise. Show each groups' work as the rest of the class sits in audience position.

Extracurricular Activities

- Decorate balloons with a face and blow them up to create a Humpty Dumpty face.

- Read other popular nursery rhymes.

- Invite children to bring in their own nursery rhyme books to share and read.

- Make or play with hobbyhorses.

- Discuss how soldiers used to ride on horses at different times in history.

- Find out which countries are governed by a monarchy.

- Make your own jigsaw puzzle by using an A4 laminated photo of the children or the class.

- Activities such as rolling down hills, along the grass, on the carpet or on a rug.

- Carry and weigh buckets of water. Explore volume and estimating. How many cups will fill the bucket?

Nursery Rhymes 2

Resources

- 'Baa Baa Black Sheep'.
- 'Hey Diddle Diddle'.
- Five scarves or squares of material.
- Extra scarves to use as simple costume pieces (optional).
- A chair for each student.

WARM-UP
Guess the Animal

Ask the children to sit in a circle or in the audience position. Select one child to make the sound of an animal. (The child can either enter the performance space or remain seated.) The rest of the children have to try and guess the animal. You can whisper the following suggestions:

o dog
o cat
o mouse
o bird
o cow
o pig
o horse
o lion
o rooster
o snake

Try to conclude this activity with

o sheep

'Baa Baa Black Sheep'

With the children still in the circle or the audience position, ask them if they know a nursery rhyme with a sheep? When the children have completed their suggestions, sing the nursery rhyme 'Baa Baa Black Sheep'. After singing the nursery rhyme, identify and discuss the different terms in the rhyme such as master, dame and lane.

Character Statues

Ask the children to stand and find a place of their own in the room. When the children are settled use the following instructions with them:

• *Can you show me a frozen statue of a sheep?*

• *Good statues, everyone, I like the way you are very still.*

- *When I clap my hands can you bring it to life?*

Clap your hands and allow the students a few moments to explore being a sheep.

- *Good, and freeze.*
- *Can you show me a frozen statue of a master?*

Clap your hands and allow the students a few moments to explore being a master.

- *Good, and freeze.*
- *Can you show me a frozen statue of a dame?*

Clap your hands and allow the students a few moments to explore being a dame.

- *Good, and freeze.*
- *Can you show me a frozen statue of a little boy or girl?*

Clap your hands and allow the students a few moments to explore being a little boy or girl.

- *Good, and freeze.*
- *Excellent work, everyone!*

FOCUS
Performing 'Baa Baa Black Sheep'

Sit the children in the audience position. Select 4 children to play the roles of the master, the dame, little boy or girl and the black sheep.

Ask the rest of the class to sing through 'Baa Baa Black Sheep' whilst the performers present the rhyme. For older children, add a line for each character. For example: as the sheep moves to each character to give them a bag of wool, the characters could say 'Thank you, sheep' or 'Thank you, sheep, I will use this wool to knit a jumper.'

If you have a large group, select 2 or more children to play each character. Encourage the children to face the audience. When each group has finished, ask the performers to take a bow and ask the audience to give them a round of applause. Don't force any unwilling child to present work, but make sure any such children are active members of the audience (that is, they watch the performance and applaud their peers).

You may want to finish the drama experience here, go to the extension activities or continue with the next part of the lesson if time permits.

'Hey Diddle Diddle'

Ask the children to sit in a circle. When the children are settled, ask them to think of other nursery rhymes that have animals. The children will call out a number of nursery rhymes.

- *Can you tell me which one has a cat, a dog and a cow that jumps over the moon?*
- *That's right, it is 'Hey Diddle Diddle'. Let's all sing the nursery rhyme together.*

Sing the nursery rhyme 'Hey Diddle Diddle' with the children.

'Hey Diddle Diddle' Character Statues

Ask the children to stand and find a place of their own in the room. When the children are settled use the following instructions with them:

• *Can you show me a frozen statue of a dog?*

• *Good statues, everyone, I like the way you are very still.*

• *When I clap my hands can you bring it to life?*

Clap your hands and allow the students a few moments to explore being a dog.

• *Good, and freeze.*

• *Can you show me a frozen statue of a cat?*

Clap your hands and allow the students a few moments to explore being a cat.

• *Good, and freeze.*

• *Can you show me a frozen statue of a cow?*

Clap your hands and allow the students a few moments to explore being a cow.

• *Good, and freeze.*

• *Can you show me a frozen statue of a dish?*

Clap your hands and allow the students a few moments to explore being a dish.

• *Good, and freeze.*

• *Can you show me a frozen statue of a spoon?*

Clap your hands and allow the students a few moments to explore being a spoon.

• *Good, and freeze.*

• *Excellent work, everyone!*

Performing 'Hey Diddle Diddle'

Ask the children to get into the audience position. Use scarves or squares of material to define the space for five characters. You may also like to use the scarves as simple costume pieces. For example: tie the scarf to become a cape, a scarf, a belt, a skirt

245

or a hood. Select some children to become the characters: the dog, the cat, cow, dish and spoon. Discuss with the children how you will represent the moon. Ask the children to sing the nursery rhyme as the performers do the actions. At the end, ask the performers to take a bow as the audience gives them a round of applause. Swap the children over to ensure they all get a turn to present in front of the audience.

FINISH

Play the game 'I'm Looking For'. Ask the children to sit on chairs. The teacher stands in the middle of the circle and proceeds as follows:

- *I'm looking for someone:*
  - *with long hair*
  - *who likes chocolate*
  - *who has been to the city/country*
  - *who has a brother*
  - *who is wearing the colour red*
  - *who has been on a bus*
  - *who has had a piece of fruit today*
  - *who likes to climb*

A child who says yes to any of the questions must stand and quickly move to a different chair in the circle.

To extend the activity, or with more experienced children, play the game as above, but select one child to stand in the middle of the circle to ask the question. When the other children begin to move, the selected child tries to find a seat. If successful, a different child will be left in the centre of the circle.

Extension

Divide the class into pairs or small groups and ask them improvise a short scene that uses animals as the characters. The scene must explore the theme of 'difference'. For example:

- The horse won't play with the sheep because of his curly 'hair'.

- The white sheep feels isolated because all the other sheep in the paddock are black.

- The dog doesn't like the cat's meow.

- The ducks don't want to share the pond with the pig because he doesn't have feathers.

Ask each group to find a solution to each problem in their scene. Give each group 5–10 minutes to plan and practise. Sit the children in audience position and ask the groups to perform their scenes, one by one.

Extracurricular Activities

- Farm excursion or visit.
- Wool craft: make pompoms, collage or weaving using wool.
- Draw or paint sheep and decorate with cotton wool.
- Dye plain or white wool using fabric or food dyes.
- Invite someone to come in and knit for the children to watch.
- 'Wear a knitted item to school' day.
- Read appropriate books with farm animals as the central characters or those that explore differences.
- Discuss dairy products. Have a 'dairy feast' (assuming none of your students are lactose intolerant!).
- Discuss cultural differences in humans such as skin colours, traditional foods, housing and language.
- Invite the children to bring in photos of their families. Discuss differences and similarities.
- 'Spot the difference' activities.

Sing a Song of Sixpence

Resources

- A drum.
- A copy of 'Sing a Song of Sixpence' – preferably with illustrations.
- Simple costume pieces, such as crowns for the king and queen, aprons for the maids and some black cloaks or a large piece of black fabric for the blackbirds.

WARM-UP
Walking to the Beat

Ask the children to find their own space in the room. When the children are settled, use the following instructions:

- *I'm going to use a drum to beat a simple rhythm. Can you move around the space walking to the beat of the drum?*

- *What will happen if I speed up the drum beats? I like the way you have varied how you walk to the faster beat.*

- *How will you change if I play a slow beat? I like the way you have changed your walk to the slower beat.*

- *Can you listen and change your walk as I play different beats?*

Vary the tempo (speed) and ask the children to move around with different qualities, for example: light steps, heavy steps, fast, slow, like they are sneaking around, like they are important, like they are in a hurry. Gradually bring the tempo back to a simple beat and the children's natural walk.

Group Shape

Ask the children to move into the centre of the room. When the children are settled use the following instructions:

- *I'm going to slowly count backwards from ten to one.*

- *As I count you must work together as a group, using your bodies to make the shape of a... castle!*

- *Ready, go. Ten... Nine... Eight... Great work, everybody, hold your position.*

- *I'm going to take a photo so you can see your great work.*

Either mime taking a photo, or take a real photo to show the children how their castle looks.

Royal Character Warm-up

Ask the children to find their own space in the room. When the children are settled, ask them to start walking around the room in their natural walk. Remind the children there is no running and no touching anyone else. When the children are focused, use the following instructions:

- *As we move around the room, we are going to become different characters.*

- *I am going to call out a character and give you some ideas about how you might become this character.*

- *Can you show me a king? Let's imagine we are the king. Can you take large steps? Can you breathe in and broaden your shoulders? You are very important. Can you put on your big, fancy cloak? Can you put on your golden crown? Can you put your nose up in the air? Can you say, 'How do you do?' Kings, let's all sit and count our big pile of money. Now take a big breath and blow that one away.*

- *Can you show me a queen? Now let's imagine we are the queen. Can you put on your long fancy dress? Can you put on your sparkling, beautiful cloak? Can you take careful steps? The queen loves to eat bread and honey. Queens have very polite manners. We are going to sit down and have some lovely bread and honey for our afternoon tea. Let's use our very best manners when we eat. Let's all say, 'How do you do?' Now take a big breath and blow that one away.*

- *Can you show me a maid? And now let's all become the maid. Can you tie on your apron? We are very busy. There's lots of housework to do. Let's all do the dishes, and now we have to sweep the floors, wipe the benches, do the cleaning, the cooking and the washing. It's tiring being this busy! Can you wipe your brow? And now we have to hang out the washing on the washing line. And breathe in and blow that one away.*

- *Can you show me a blackbird? Let's become the blackbird. Let's rest in our nest. Can you stretch out your wings? Show me your black feathers. Let's fly out of the nest and peck for food. The blackbird likes to sit in a tree and look down at the people. What sound do blackbirds make? Good, blow it away.*

FOCUS
Sing a Song of Sixpence

Ask the children to sit in a circle. When the children are settled, sing the nursery rhyme, 'Sing a Song of Sixpence'. Encourage the children to participate vocally by repeating some of the lines, or reading along with you. Invite the children to play all the characters in the story as you say the lines together.

After going through the nursery rhyme, ask the children to find their own place in the room. When the children are settled use the following instructions:

- *We are going to explore the characters in the nursery rhyme.*

- *Can you show me a frozen statue of the king? When I clap my hands, the king will come to life and count his money.*

Repeat the activity for each of the characters. For older children you may wish to encourage them to improvise lines for the characters for example:

> KING (*counting*): One, two, three, four, five, six, seven, eight, nine, ten. I'm the richest man in the whole kingdom.

> QUEEN (*eating*): Mmmm, delicious! Bread and honey is my favourite.

> MAID (*doing housework*): Busy, busy, busy. A maid's work is never done.

> BLACKBIRD (*flying*): Squawk, Squawk! I'm a clever blackbird.

For younger children, you may wish to use the first sentence for each character from the nursery rhyme.

Performing Sing a Song of Sixpence

31

Ask the children to sit in the audience position. If your class is small (8–12 children), they will all be able to present together. If your class is larger (15–25), some will remain as the audience whilst the others perform. Select children to be the characters of the story: king, queen, maid and 3–8 children as the blackbirds. As the teacher in role, narrate the nursery rhyme and encourage the children to mime the story and to improvise lines for the characters. Encourage confident, loud speaking, facing the audience, attention to detail in the miming and remembering the text and lines.

You may wish to add simple costume pieces such as a crown for the king and queen, aprons for the maids, black cloaks for the birds. You may also wish to begin with the blackbirds under a piece of black fabric. As the narrator, you can lift the piece of fabric when the pie is 'opened'.

When the children have completed the performance, remind the actors take a bow and the audience to give a round of applause. If necessary, swap the audience and the actors or rotate the characters, so the children have an opportunity to play a different role.

Repeat until everyone has had a turn at performing.

SING A SONG OF SIXPENCE

FINISH

Play the game 'Kings Treasure' (page 37). You play the role of king, standing at one end of the room facing away from the class with a 'treasure' behind you, at your feet. The children line up along the opposite wall and attempt to sneak up on the king to steal the treasure. When the king turns around, the children must freeze. The king returns anyone caught moving back to the start. When a child steals the treasure, he or she must run back to the start without being caught by the king.

Extension

Involve more children in the performance by having more than one king, queen and maid. Create new characters such as princesses, royal guards, cooks, bird hunters, narrators and other animals. Build music, instruments and more complex costumes and sets into the performance.

Extracurricular Activities

- Make a pie with real ingredients, or recycled materials, playdough or mud.

- Count money: use tokens or toy coins. Make piles or groups of coins. Explore simple math exercises.

- Create an indoor or outdoor washing line. Peg up dolls' clothes or small pieces of fabric. Wash before hanging if desired.

- Draw a blackbird. Explore and investigate different kinds of birds.

- Host a royal party with real or pretend food.

- Make crowns by stapling a piece of long card to fit around a child's head. Decorate with sequins or scraps of paper.

- Explore the sense of smell. Fill small containers with different foods, spices or plants. Select one child to be blindfolded and smell each container. The child must identify the smell, or simply categorise into 'good' and 'bad' smells.

The Teddy Bears' Picnic

Resources

- 'The Teddy Bears' Picnic' music.
- 'The Teddy Bears' Picnic' lyrics.
- Tambourine.
- One coloured scarf or square of fabric for each two children.
- A large picnic rug (optional).

WARM-UP
Using Our Hands

Ask the children to sit in a circle. When the children are settled, use the following instructions:

- *Can you show me your hands?*
- *Can you make your hands move fast?*
- *Can you make your hands move slowly?*
- *Can you make your hands look strong?*
- *Can you make your hands look wobbly?*
- *Can you make your hands look tired?*
- *Can you make your hands look crazy!*
- *Can you make your hands look sneaky?*
- *Good, let's creep them down on the floor.*
- *Can you creep them on to your lap, your tummy, your shoulders?*
- *Can you creep them under your arms and give yourself a tickle!*
- *Can you creep them behind your back?*

Sneaky Walks

Ask the children to stand up where they are. Remind the children that there is no running and they should not touch anybody else during the activity. When the children are ready use the following instructions:

- *Let's see if you can find a sneaky way to move around. I like the way you all look very sneaky while you move!*
- *Can you find a sneaky face to match the sneaky way you are moving? I really like your sneaky faces.*
- *I like these sneaky moves! I can't even hear you moving!*
- *Now freeze!*

Teddy Bear Characters

Play 'The Teddy Bears' Picnic' music throughout this warm-up. Ask the children to find their own space in the room. When they are settled, use the following instructions:

- *Let's imagine we are going to become teddy bears.*

- *Imagine:*

  o *you are growing some fur*
  o *your tummy is getting bigger*
  o *your hands are turning into paws*
  o *your ears are growing round and furry*
  o *you are turning into a teddy bear*

- *Let's be a:*

  o *big bear*
  o *small bear*
  o *fat bear*
  o *floppy bear*
  o *grumpy bear*
  o *hungry bear*

'The Teddy Bears' Picnic' song

Ask the children to sit in a circle. When the children settle ask them to sing the song 'The Teddy Bears' Picnic'. After they have finished, ask the children what they imagine when they sing it. Questions you ask them may include:

- *What do you think the forest looks like?*

- *What would the teddy bears eat on their picnic?*

Discuss

Sit the children in a circle, or on the big picnic rug. Talk about the teddy bears that the children have. Questions you may like to ask could include:

- *Do you have a teddy bear?*
- *What does it look like?*
- *Do you cuddle your teddy bear?*
- *Does your teddy bear have a name?*
- *Would your teddy bear like to come to school for a visit?*

FOCUS
The Woods

Ask the children to find their own space in the room. When the children are settled use the following instructions:

- *Guess what, teddy bears, we are going to visit the woods today.*
- *We are going to make the woods in our classroom.*
- *Can you crouch down in the smallest position that you can?*
- *I'm going to count slowly from one to ten.*
- *When you hear me shake the tambourine can you 'grow' into a forest?*
- *That was very good. Let's try it again.*
- *Can you grow into a different-shaped tree this time?*
- *Well done, everyone. We are now the woods.*

Divide the class in half. Ask one half to spread out in the performance space as the forest. The rest become teddy bears and wait on the audience mat. Play the music. Ask the teddy bears to enter the 'forest' and creep around the trees, hiding behind a tree then moving quickly to another one. The trees stay as still as possible. Swap the groups over and repeat the activity.

The Picnic

Ask all the children to find a place to 'fall asleep'. When the children are asleep, read the first verse of 'The Teddy Bears' Picnic'. After reading it, use the following story with the children:

- *Wake up, teddy bears! Today is our special day. The day of our picnic.*
- *Have a big stretch and rub your eyes.*
- *We have to pack our favourite foods for the picnic.*
- *I'm going to pack some biscuits, what are you going to pack?*

Ask all the children to share with the group what they are going to pack.

Give one scarf between two children as the picnic rug or use one big rug to share.

- *The teddy bears walked up the big hill, and ran down the other side. They climbed over the gate and through the rocks. Finally they went into the woods. They were sneaking through the woods, carrying their picnic baskets. They looked around for the perfect spot. When they found it they spread out their picnic rugs.*

Children spread out scarves. When the children have spread out the scarves and prepared for the picnic, discuss with them what they are eating. Encourage them to mime and improvise in character with their peers. It doesn't matter if they are all speaking at once. The dialogue may go something like this:

TEACHER: I'm going to eat some apples.

CHILDREN: I'm going to eat some _____.

After eating the picnic, read the second verse of the song to the children. Play the music and ask the children to play in the woods.

After the children have had some time to play in the woods, ask them to form a circle. When the children are settled, use the following instructions:

- *Let's all hold hands.*
- *Let's all skip in, in, in.*
- *Let's all skip, out, out, out.*

Repeat.

- *Oh dear, the teddy bears have been playing all day and now they are very tired.*
- *Have a big yawn. Find a place to fall asleep.*
- *Let's pretend we are the mummies and daddies. Stand up and walk into the woods.*
- *Can you see your teddy bear? Pick it up and give it a big bear hug. Take your teddy bear back home.*

Children mime picking up their bears. Ask the children to fall asleep in their 'beds', using their scarves as the beds. Repeat the last lines of the chorus.

FINISH
Musical Mats

Spread the scarves around the space and play some music. As the music plays, the children dance around the scarves. When the music stops children must stand on a scarf. Remove a scarf after each round until there are only three left. Children must find a way to stand on the scarves in small groups.

Extension

Divide the class into small groups and allocate each group a verse of the song. Children can choose how they want to interpret the verse. They may want to use chorus (speaking at the same time), narration, mime, group movement or a combination of these. Encourage use of levels (high, medium and low), and encourage them to face the audience. If they are using sound, encourage loud and clear voices. After rehearsing their scenes, ask the children to sit in the audience position. The children take it in turns to perform their scenes. Remind the children to take a bow when they have finished performing and remind the audience to applaud the performers.

Extracurricular Activities

- Draw or paint a teddy bear picture.
- Write a teddy bear adventure story.
- Have a teddy bears' picnic, indoors or outdoors.
- Bring your teddy bear to class.
- Make a teddy bear face with a paper plate.
- Make a teddy bear using playdough and a bear cookie cutter.
- Have a teddy bear tea party, invite your teddy bear. Use pretend food.
- Use the children's bears and classify them using different criteria, for example: size, weight, colour or the length of their fur.

- Make teddy bear ears – paper strip or headband and staple ears on.
- Research and discuss different types of bears from around the world.

The Three Little Pigs

Resources

- 'Here's a House'.
- *The Three Little Pigs*.
- Collection of instruments (optional).

WARM-UP
Warm-up Circle

Begin with the 'Warm-up Circle' (see *Let's Get Started!*, page 2).

Here's a House

Ask the children to sit in a circle. When the children are settled, use the following instructions:

- *We are going to build some houses today.*
- *I'm going to need some big, strong helpers.*
- *What are some things that we need to build a house?*
- *What shall we start with?*
- *It might be a good idea to start our house with a floor.*

Sing the song 'Here's a House' with the children (you can find this online if you don't know it already). Repeat the song with actions. You may also like to sing the song standing up so the crash is even more dramatic.

Pig Characters

Ask the children to stand up and spread out in the space. When the children are settled, use the following instructions.

- *We are going to imagine that we are becoming pigs. Imagine that:*
  - *your skin is turning pink*
  - *your tummies are getting bigger*
  - *you have a little curly tail growing out of your bum!*
- *Now little pigs, we have a busy day today. We are going to build a house.*
- *We're going to make a house built entirely out of straw.*

- *Who can find some straw? There's a lot around here. Come on, help me collect some straw.*

Mime finding bundles of straw around the classroom. If a child collects a real prop, remind them that we are 'just pretending', that we are 'miming'.

- *Now that we have a big bundle, let's start building.*

- *We are going to start with the floor. Well done, that looks great.*

- *Now what is next? The walls! Use some more straw and help me build the walls. Wow, that looks fantastic.*

- *Now what do we need to do to finish the house? We have the floor and the walls. That's right, the roof! Get some more straw, now can you reach right up to the top and build the roof. Beautiful! We have finished our house of straw.*

- *Oh dear, I can feel a very strong wind. Can you hear it?*

Encourage the children to make the sound of the wind.

- *Oh no! Our little house of straw has fallen down.*

- *Oh well, let's try building a stronger house.*

- *We can use some sticks!*

Repeat the building sequence with the children using sticks, then repeat again using bricks.

Wolf Characters

Ask the children to stand and find a place of their own. When the children are settled, use the following instructions:

- *Let's imagine that you are growing fur all over your bodies.*

- *Imagine your shoulders are coming forward and you are growing long claws.*

- *What's happening to your teeth? That's right, they are getting bigger and sharper.*

- *You have a big bushy tail.*

- *Now can you show me how you can creep around the space?*
- *Show me how hungry you are.*
- *You have turned into a big... bad... wolf!*
- *Come on, wolves, I can smell something yummy.*

Encourage the children to start sniffing.

- *It smells like a delicious fat little pig.*
- *There he is.*

Gesture to centre of the room. Remind the children that they should remain in role as the wolf.

- *The pig is hiding in that house made of straw.*
- *Let's go and knock on the door.*

Read the following lines from *The Three Little Pigs*:

> WOLF: Little pig, little pig, let me in!
>
> PIG: Not by the hair of my chinny-chin-chin!
>
> WOLF: Then I'll huff and I'll puff and I'll blow your house in!

As the children use the dialogue they will need to switch between the two characters of the wolf and the pig continually. Avoid lots of movement around the space, but encourage the children to make the change by alternating levels (the wolf standing, the pig crouching down), changing their voices (the wolf has a low, growly voice, the pig's voice is high and soft) and their facial expression (the wolf looks hungry and dangerous, the pig looks frightened).

- *Freeze.*
- *Let's all become the wolf again.*
- *Now let's knock on this little house made of sticks.*

Repeat the dialogue at each house. When the wolf attempts to blow the brick house down he gets exhausted. It will be up to your own discretion as to how you narrate the ending. In many traditional versions of the story, the wolf climbs down the chimney and lands in a boiling pot of water. In other versions, the wolf leaves the third house 'never to be seen again'.

FOCUS

Telling the Story of The Three Little Pigs

Ask the children to sit in the audience position. Select some children to play Pig #1, Pig #2, Pig #3, House #1, House #2, House #3, and the Wolf. If your group is small, you may not need children to play the role of the houses. If your group is large, you may want to select some children to be the orchestra. Sit them on the side of the stage and give them some instruments such as drums to accompany the pigs walking, and shakers for the creeping wolf.

Ask the houses to stand on stage with their legs out wide and arms reaching up, palms together, or hands on hip. If your class is large, you may select two or more children to create the shape of the house. Ask a pig to sit in front of each house. The wolf can be seated to the side of the three houses and pigs. As each house is blown down, its pig moves to the next house.

Narrate the story as the children act it out. (For older children, select a few children to be the narrators.) Encourage the children to say the dialogue on their own, speak loudly and clearly, face the audience and remain in character.

At the end of the story, ask the actors to face the audience and take a bow. Ask the audience to give the actors a round of applause.

Repeat the story until all of the children have performed.

FINISH
Wolves and Pigs

Ask the children to stand in a circle holding hands. Select one child to be the pig standing inside the circle, and select another child to be the wolf, standing outside the circle. On your command, the wolf must try to catch the pig. The rest of the children can choose when they raise their arms to let either the pig or wolf to run under. When the wolf tags the pig, select two different children. (If the game is going on too long, invite those children to 'have a rest' and select two more children.)

Extension

Divide the class into small groups. Ask them to present the story of *The Three Little Pigs* with a 'twisted ending'. For example: the pigs are bad and the wolf is the victim, the wolf only wants to borrow a cup of sugar, the brick house falls over, the wolf has very bad breath and the pigs give him a toothbrush. Allow a few minutes for the children to plan and practise. Show each group's work one at a time.

Extracurricular Activities

- Build houses from small boxes or other recycled materials.
- Draw or paint a pig or wolf.
- Create a paper-plate pig mask.
- Make curly pipe-cleaner tails.
- Make an egg carton snout by attaching some elastic to a cup from an egg carton.
- Discuss good table manners.
- Make a piggy bank and discuss good saving habits.
- Read any books with a pig or a wolf as central characters.
- Look at houses from around the world and discuss different building materials.

The Very Hungry Caterpillar

Resources

- *The Very Hungry Caterpillar* by Eric Carle.
- A scarf or square of fabric for each child.
- Relaxation music.
- A long piece of fabric.

WARM-UP
Caterpillars, Pears and Cheese

Ask the children to find their own space in the room. When they are settled, use the following instructions:

- *Can you make yourself small? Can you roll yourself up like a little ball?*

- *Can you make yourself tall? Can you stretch right up with your hands and go on to your tippy-toes?*

- *Can you make yourself small? Can you roll yourself into a little ball again like a tiny little plum? Good.*

- *Now I'm going to give you some more shapes. Make yourself into:*
  - *a strawberry, with spiky leaves on top*
  - *a pear with a stalk*
  - *a long, thin sausage*
  - *a thin slice of cheese*

Repeat some of the foods from the book and ask the children to make the shapes either in pairs or in groups of 3 or 4. For example:

- *With your partner, can you work together to make the shape of a lollipop?*

- *In your group, can you work together to make the shape of a slice of cake?*

FOCUS
The Very Hungry Caterpillar

Ask the children to sit in front of you. When the children are settled, read *The Very Hungry Caterpillar*. Encourage the children to repeat the chorus lines as you read the story, for example: 'but he was still hungry'. Also encourage the children to use gestures with their hands to show the caterpillar growing bigger and bigger and to count the pieces of fruit.

Ask the children to find their own space in the room. Once the children are settled, ask them to roll themselves into a little egg.

Cover each child with a scarf. Play the relaxation music and narrate the main parts of the story. You can either read directly from the book, or use it as a stimulus. You also may like to divide the class into two groups, with one group being the audience while the other performs, then swap them over.

For older or more experienced children, repeat the story but select one child to be the hungry caterpillar and divide the rest of the class into the various fruit and vegetables.

The 'caterpillar' can crawl through the legs of the other children as it eats the food, or mime eating while the others (being eaten) join on behind it. If the children who are being the food are using scarves as costumes, the hungry caterpillar could take the scarf to mimic eating the food, stuffing it into their own clothes to show they are getting bigger. These variations will depend on your group size, your time limits and the skill level of your class.

A Giant Caterpillar

Ask all (or half) the class to stand in a line. Place the long fabric over their heads and ask them to hold on to the edges of the fabric. Ask the children to move around the space, weaving around in all directions. Keep swapping the leader of the line. Repeat until all, or most, of the children have been the 'leader'.

FINISH
Musical Mats

Spread scarves around the room as 'flowers'. Play some music and ask the children to fly around the room as butterflies. When the music stops, the butterflies must quickly land on a flower. Take away a flower after each round. Either eliminate the slowest butterfly or ask the children to share the flowers. Extend the game by asking the children to alternate between flying butterflies and crawling caterpillars.

Extension

Build the story into a performance by giving each child a line from the story, a food to be, and build a 'butterfly dance' as an ending. Or divide the class into small groups and ask them to present a short scene about 'The adventure of the very tiny caterpillar', 'The day of the Butterfly Ball' or 'When the caterpillar met the spider'. Ask the children to add a moment of slow motion or a moment of fast-forward. Discuss how the use of time impacts the performance.

Extracurricular Activities

- Egg-carton caterpillar: cut a line of cups from an egg carton. Paint and decorate. Add some eyes on one end and thread two pipe-cleaners through for antennae.

- Make butterfly pictures: fold a piece of paper in half. Paint some wings on one side of the paper, then fold in half so the wings are printed on the other side as you unfold the paper. Discuss symmetry.

- Have a hungry caterpillar feast, eating the foods from the story.

- Glue pompoms together to make caterpillars, or thread some beads onto pipe-cleaners.

- Discuss life cycles of animals and metamorphosis.

- Make a class-size caterpillar by asking each child

to decorate a paper circle and gluing them together on to a large sheet of paper.

- Make some butterflies by folding some paper in a concertina fold and then wrap a pipe-cleaner around the centre for the body. Spread out the wings and decorate. Hang them from fishing line around the room.

- Visit a zoo or local park to observe butterflies and caterpillars. Read appropriate literature and picture books.

- Make butterfly cakes: slice the top off a cup cake and halve it. Add cream to the base and stick the cut halves in the cream on an angle as butterfly wings. Dust with icing sugar.

- Find a cocoon and bring it into class.

THE VERY HUNGRY CATERPILLAR

The Wheels on the Bus

Resources

- 'Ring a Ring o' Roses'.
- 'The Wheels on the Bus'.
- Chairs, mats, cushions or scarves to make bus seats.
- Conductor's hat for teacher in role (optional).

WARM-UP
Follow the Leader

Ask the children to walk all around the space without talking or touching anybody else. Ask them to slowly change their walk into a 'sneaky' walk. Ask them each to select another child secretly and follow that child. Eventually, there will be one or two lines of children moving around the space. Repeat the activity several times.

Circles

Ask the children to find their own space in the room. When the children are settled, use the following instructions:

- *A circle is a shape we see all the time.*
- *Let's look around our classroom.*
- *Can you see any circles?*

Walk around the room with the children looking for and identifying circles.

- *We are going to make some circles with different parts of our bodies.*
- *Make a circle with your:*
  - o *fingers*
  - o *arms*
  - o *legs*
  - o *whole bodies*
- *Now can you make a circle with a partner?*
- *Let's join all together to make a big group.*
- *Can we make a circle all together?*

As a group, sing the song 'Ring a Ring o' Roses' and act out the actions in the song.

Discuss

Ask the children to sit in a circle and discuss their experiences of being on a bus. Questions you may like to ask might include:

• *Have you been on a bus?*

• *Where did you go?*

Sing through the first verse of the song 'The Wheels on the Bus' with the children.

FOCUS
The Bus

With the children still sitting in a circle, use the following instructions:

- *We are going to go on a bus today.*
- *Before we go on our bus, let's sing the bus song.*
- *Sing the first verse of 'The Wheels on the Bus'.*
- *Let's see if we can make a bus in our classroom.*

Lead the children in making a bus. Use chairs, mats, cushions or scarves to make the seats. After making the bus, read the following:

- *Here comes the bus!*
- *Have you all got your tickets?*
- *The doors are opening.*
- *Let's get on board.*

Sit at the front of the 'bus' and role-play as the bus driver. You may like to wear a conductor's hat to help you get into role. You will need to be prepared to step in and out of role throughout the class. Ask the children to line up behind each other. Mime collecting tickets from each child. You may like to sing 'The conductor on the bus says, "Tickets please."' as you collect the tickets and the children move along the bus. Make sure each child is seated after you collect his or her ticket.

Once the children are seated on the bus, use the following dialogue:

- *Okay, everyone, are you ready to go?*
- *Let's start the engine.*

All children make the sound of the engine.

- *And off we go!*
- *Uh-oh, look up at those dark clouds. It's starting to rain!*
- *We had better switch on the windscreen wipers.*

Sing the wiper verse ('The wipers on the bus go swish, swish, swish') with the children.

- *The rain has stopped.*

- *Now I can see a mother duck and all her babies trying to cross the road. Look out ducks. How can we let them know we are coming?*

    CHILDREN: Beep the horn!

Sing the horn verse ('The horn on the bus goes beep, beep, beep').

- *Hold on, everyone!*
- *It looks like we have turned on to the bumpy road!*
- *Hold on while the bus goes up and down over the bumps.*

Sing the people verse ('The people on the bus go up and down').

- *Sorry about all those bumps, everyone.*
- *Oh dear. The bumps have woken up all the babies on the bus and they are starting to cry!*

Sing the babies verse ('The babies on the bus go waa, waa, waa').

- *Quick, mummies/daddies/parents.*
- *Can you try to rock the babies back to sleep?*

Sing the mummies/daddies/parents verse ('The mummies on the bus go shh, shh, shh').

- *Phew! The babies have gone back to sleep.*
- *And guess what? We are here! Did you all enjoy your ride on the bus today?*
- *Thank you, passengers. See you next time!*

You may like to extend this activity by arriving at different destinations along the way between the verses of the song. Invite all the passengers to get off the bus and explore the new location (such as the shops, a zoo, the city, a farm) then, in role as the conductor, announce that the bus is leaving soon and all passengers need to get on board.

FINISH

Ask the children to move around the space in an interesting way. Repeat the 'Follow the Leader' activity above, but this time ask the children to try and copy the way the person is moving in front of them. Also tell them to try not to get 'caught' by the person in front of them.

Extension

Divide the class into small groups and ask each group to present a scene called 'The adventure on the bus'. Encourage interesting characters and improvisation. You may want to remind the children to think up a problem to ensure their story is engaging for an audience. For more experienced children, remind them to face the audience when presenting.

Extracurricular Activities

- Go on an excursion on a local bus.
- Create a classroom bus by lining up large cardboard boxes. Decorate with paper-plate wheels. Add a horn, number plates and 'lights' using aluminium foil.
- Make a miniature bus by using a shoebox for toys to enjoy a bus ride.
- Use a box to make a ticket machine and cut up small pieces of paper for the tickets.
- Make a bus stop – indoors or outdoors.
- Discuss different forms of public transport.
- Read books about buses and other means of public transport.
- Make an egg-carton bus.
- Find pictures of different kinds of buses from around the world.

Where the Wild Things Are

Resources

- A tambourine or shaker.
- *Where the Wild Things Are* by Maurice Sendak.
- Jungle music or something with a tribal sound.
- A collection scarves or squares of fabric, instruments or music.
- Relaxation music.
- A large piece of fabric.

WARM-UP
Growing into Shapes

Ask the children to spread out and find a space of their own. When the children are settled, use the following instructions:

- *Can you imagine that you are a tiny seed of imagination? Can you make yourself very tiny?*

- *Now as I make this sound, can your seed begin to grow? Let your imagination grow into a big, sparkling, glowing star of imagination.*

Use an instrument such as a tambourine or shaker and count slowly from one to ten. Ask the children to 'grow' into a tall and interesting position.

- *Now let's shrink down again. You are just a tiny speck of imagination.*

- *When you hear the sound, use your imagination and grow into a new interesting shape.*

Continue to alternate between small and tall shapes.

Wild Characters

Ask the children to find their own place in the room. When they are ready, use the following instructions:

- *Can you move around the space to the sound of the beat?*

- *Can you move:*
    - *slow?*
    - *fast?*
    - *soft?*
    - *loud?*
    - *slow and loud?*
    - *fast and soft?*
    - *fast and loud?*
    - *slow and soft?*

- *Excellent, now can you show me your natural walk?*

- *Now as you are moving around, imagine that you are getting bigger.*

- *Your nails are growing longer.*
- *Your teeth are growing sharper.*
- *Your eyes are getting wider.*
- *You are growing horns on your head.*
- *You are growing fur all over your body.*
- *You have big shoulders and a scary face.*
- *You have become something wild.*
- *A WILD THING!*
- *Can you roar like a Wild Thing?*
- *Show me your claws, your teeth and your big round eyes.*
- *I know a story about Wild Things, do you know a story about Wild Things?*

Story

Ask the children to sit in front of you, making sure they can all see the book. Read the story *Where the Wild Things Are*. Encourage lots of active participation, while still remaining seated. For example: the children can use their hands to grow into a forest, make the sounds of the waves with their voices, repeat some of the lines or rock from side to side on their boats.

Discuss

After reading the book, discuss the story with the children. Questions you may like to ask include:

- *Did Max really go to the place where the Wild Things are?*
- *Is there such a place? Was it just a dream?*
- *Do you ever imagine that your bedroom is turning into a different place?*
- *Would you like the visit the place of the Wild Things today?*

FOCUS
Going Where the Wild Things Are

Ask the children to spread out and find a space of their own. Narrate the story *Where the Wild Things Are* as the children act out the various sequences. The children will be continually changing character, from Max to the Wild Things. They will also be moving into the various shapes and environments from the story. As you are reading the book, the children will explore:

- Pretending to be naughty as Max.
- The angry mother calling Max a Wild Thing.
- Grumpy as Max – returning to room.
- Growing into the forest – small to tall (use the tambourine).
- The waves – joining hands in a circle. Moving in and out. 'Shhh' sounds.
- The boat. Individually, in pairs or as one big group.
- Max sailing in the boat.
- The Wild Things. Repeat the actions (roar their terrible roars, for instance).
- Max being brave – staring into their yellow eyes.
- Moving around in the 'Wild Rumpus' – use jungle music.
- The Wild Things sleeping.
- Max being lonely and sad.
- Max trying to sneak away.
- The Wild Things waking up: 'Oh Please don't go…', etc.
- Max sailing away in the boat.
- The waves – join hands in a circle and move in and out making 'shhh' sounds.
- Max sleeping – then waking and eating the supper.

After going through the story once, repeat the story. This time, select one child to be Max and another to play the role of the mother. The other children will play the role of the Wild Things, and create the images of the forest, the ocean and the boat. Use a collection of fabric, instruments and music to help recreate the story. For example: you might encourage the children to use scarves to create the forest, wave them up and down for the waves of the ocean, or to use as a cape to become a Wild Thing. You can choose to narrate the story while the children are exploring the actions and movements, or select a few children to tell the story in their own words. Depending on the size of your class, you may choose to have some children sitting in the audience. Allow time for the children to swap between audience member and performer.

Wild Rumpus Musical Statues

Play some music and ask the children to move around as Wild Things. When the music stops, ask the children to find an interesting shape to freeze in. If any Wild Things move or wobble, ask them to step out to help become a judge, watching for any other Wild Things that move when they should be statues.

FINISH
Relaxation

Play the relaxation music. Invite the children to lie down in a comfortable position. Stretch a large piece of fabric over the children. You will need to use an assistant or ask a child to hold the other end. Gently lift the fabric up and down over the resting children. When the children are settled, use the following instructions with the children:

- *Close your eyes and breathe in and out deeply.*
- *Listen to the music.*
- *Let your imaginations begin to grow.*
- *Can you imagine an adventure of your own?*
- *Your adventure might begin in a forest, or the ocean or even on a cloud.*
- *Relax and let your imaginations take you on an adventure.*

Give the children a few minutes to rest. Ask them about their adventures when you sit them up. You may like to record these for further use in drama, art or storytelling.

Extension

Choreograph a Wild Rumpus dance and include a line of dialogue for each child. Get the children to stand in a circle and play the jungle music. Ask each child to do one movement. For example: a jump, a spin, hip wobble or nodding the head three times. Ensure that each child contributes and build the movements into a sequence. You can extend this activity by dividing the students into small groups and asking them to choreograph their own Wild Rumpus dance. You can suggest that they need to include a jump, a stomp, a movement in a circle and a finishing position. Extend the activity one more time by asking each Wild Thing to think of a name for their character and something which they like to do. For example: 'My name is Big Teeth and I like to eat worms' or 'I am Mr Grumpy and I never take a bath'.

Build the story *Where the Wild Things Are* into a performance by dividing the text from the story into lines for narrators. Either select 3 or 4 children to be the narrators, or a give a line to each child.

Extracurricular Activities

- Discuss dreams. Share children's dreams with the rest of the class. Ask the children to draw or paint images from their dreams. Create dream catchers.

- Have a Wild Rumpus party – discuss what foods a Wild Thing would eat.

- Write a scary story, either on your own or as a group. For example: each child thinks of one sentence.

- Make a list of scary things. Discuss which are real, which are imaginary.

- Create a forest mural – cut out children's handprints as leaves.

- Make a cardboard-box boat – sail around the world or over the ocean to imaginary lands.

- Draw or paint a Wild Thing.

- Use instruments or create some of your own using recycled materials and make a Wild Thing band.

FIVE

SEASONS

Autumn

Resources

- A long piece of blue, white or silver fabric, in a light or transparent material.
- Five mats or a collection of scarves to sit on.
- Up to five scarves for the wind.
- A collection of musical instruments: xylophones; sticks (if possible, a rainstick); a drum; cymbals or saucepan lids.
- A collection of autumn leaves, either real or cut out from coloured paper.
- Relaxation music.

WARM-UP

Hand Warm-up

Ask the children to sit in a circle. When the children are settled, use the following instructions:

- *Let's begin by warming up our hands.*
- *Can you make your hands move fast?*
- *Can you make your hands move slowly?*
- *Can you make your hands look angry? Bend your fingers and make your hands shake.*
- *Can you make your hands look shy? Hide them behind your back!*
- *Can you make your hands look excited? Wave them around.*
- *Now can you make your hands look sad? Droop them forward.*
- *Can you make your hands look strong?*
- *Can you make your hands look light? Float them up above your head.*
- *Can you make your hands look like leaves floating down from a tree?*

The Leaf Song

Remain in the circle. When the children are settled, sing the following song with the children (the tune is 'The Farmer in the Dell / in his Den'):

> Leaves are falling down, leaves are falling down,
> Flitter flutter, flitter flutter, leaves are falling down.

Repeat the song again, but this time ask the children to stand and pretend they are a leaf, holding on tightly to the tree (stretch one hand up above head). As they sing flitter flutter, ask them to float slowly down to the ground. Remaining in the circle, use the following instructions with the children. Insist on slow, gentle movements. Remind the children that there is no bumping or touching anyone else:

- *Let's stand up and hold on to the tree again. Don't let go.*
- *Oh look! Here comes the soft autumn wind. It's blowing stronger and stronger. Hold on.*
- *It's too strong now. It's time to let go.*
- *Can you float gently all around in the wind and then get lower, lower and lower until we rest on the ground?*

Repeat the activity again from the start.

Discuss

Ask the children to sit in a circle. When they are settled, discuss what they know about seasons. You may like to ask such questions as:

- *Have you heard the word 'seasons'?*
- *What does it mean?*
- *Can you name them all?*
- *What season are we in now?*
- *Do all countries have different seasons?*
- *Autumn is a beautiful time of year when some of the trees do a special magic trick. Do you know what it is?*

The children should talk about the leaves changing colour. Discuss the different colours of the leaves as they change and the experiences the children have had with them.

FOCUS
Autumn Trees

Ask the children to spread out in the space and find a place of their own. Remind them that there is no running or touching anybody else. When the children are settled, use the following instructions:

- *Now let's pretend that we are an autumn tree.*

- *Keep your feet very still and grow your roots down through the ground.*

- *Stretch out your branches.*

- *Hold on tightly to all your colourful leaves.*

- *Now the autumn wind is blowing.*

Weave through the children with the long piece of fabric. Make the sound 'shhh' as you move through the children.

- *And now it is time to let go of your leaves.*

- *Sprinkle them all over the garden to make a beautiful autumn carpet.*

- *Look at all the leaves! Let's go stomping through the big piles of leaves.*

Allow the children to mime playing in the autumn leaves.

- *Freeze.*

- *Can you make the sound of the wind?*

- *What does wind look like?*

- *Can you move around the space as the wind moves through the trees?*

An Autumn Story

Divide the children into small groups of no more than 5. Sit each group on a mat or collection of scarves around a central space. Place the large fabric in the centre for the trees. Allocate each group as follows:

- Group 1 is the wind. Give them all a scarf.

- Group 2 is rain. Give them xylophones or sticks that can be tapped against any metal or glass object. Include a rainstick if you have one.

- Group 3 is thunder. Give them a drum or ask them to stomp their feet on the ground.

- Group 4 is lightning. Give them cymbals or pot lids to crash together.

- Group 5 are autumn trees. Stand the group on the large fabric in the centre of the space. Either cut out autumn leaves from construction paper, or give them strips of coloured paper as leaves. You may also give them real autumn leaves if you have some.

- Group 6 is the audience. You only need to include this if your group is large. Explain that they will swap roles later.

If your group is small, combine groups 1 and 2, and 3 and 4. Play the autumn music. When the children are ready, narrate the following story.

- *Once upon a time, there were some very big autumn trees in a garden.*

- *The trees had been covered in beautiful bright green leaves all summer long, but now it was autumn and the trees loved this time of year.*

- *They performed their special magic trick and turned all their leaves into different colours – red, yellow, orange, brown and purple.*

- *The trees held onto their beautiful leaves, but one day the wind came to visit.*

Enter the wind. The children dance around the trees waving their scarves. After a short while ask them to return to their mat.

- *Then came the gentle rain.*

The rain children play their music and circle the trees/garden.

- *Then came the giant thunder and lightning, which lit up the sky around the garden.*

The groups of thunder and lightning play their instruments and circle the garden.

- *The trees held on to their leaves as tightly as they could, then the thunder, lightning and rain stopped.*

The children return to their mats.

- *The wind came rushing through the garden once again.*

- *The trees danced and swayed with the wind. Then they knew it was time to decorate the garden, so they let go of their leaves.*

The children let go of their leaves and sprinkle them on the large piece of fabric.

- *Now the garden was covered in a carpet of autumn leaves.*

- *And that is the story of the autumn trees.*

Remind the audience to clap and the performing children to take a bow. Swap roles and repeat the story.

FINISH

Ask the children to lie down with their eyes closed. Play the relaxation music. Hold up one end of the long fabric and use an assistant or another child to hold the other end. Gently lift the fabric up and down over the children to create a gentle 'wind'. Ask the children to imagine where the wind will go to next.

Extension

Divide the children into small groups. Ask them to present a short movement sequence that must begin with the trees holding their leaves and finish when they scatter the leaves below them. They may like to use movement, mime, dance, narrative, chorus work, instruments and scarves. Give each group 5–10 minutes to practise and then ask the children to sit in the audience position. Allow time for each group to present their movement sequence.

Extracurricular Activities

- Make an individual or class autumn tree. Paint a tree trunk and branches, or use children's forearms and hands dipped in brown paint. Use children's handprints as leaves.

- Leaf rubbings. Extend the activity to interesting texture/object rubbings.

- Leaf collecting. Sort in colour, shape, size and texture.

- Hold an autumn party – dress up in autumn colours and eat autumn-coloured food.

- Go on an excursion to the local park. Have a scavenger hunt to find particular leaves: the biggest, the smallest, or one with three different colours, for instance.

- Make stained-glass leaves using black paper and cellophane. Cut a leaf shape out of black paper and fill the shape with red, yellow and orange cellophane.

- Make a leaf garland by attaching leaves to a piece of string and hanging it across your room.

- Investigate the difference between deciduous and evergreen trees.

- Discuss the fact that many countries do not have autumn.

- Discuss the origins and celebrations of the Chinese mid-autumn festival.

Winter

Resources

- 'It's Raining, It's Pouring'.
- A winter hat, scarf, jacket and gloves, plus a chair (or mat) for each team (up to 4, depending on the size of your class).
- A long piece of fabric, preferably white or silver.
- Relaxation music.
- White or silver star-shaped or snowflake-shaped sequins.

WARM-UP
Hot and Cold Walks

Ask the children to stand and find a place of their own. Remind the children there is no running or touching anybody else. When the children are settled, use the following instructions:

- *Let's begin by walking around the space. Now, as you are moving around, I want you to imagine that it is very hot. How do we move when it is very hot? Good, I like the way you are wiping your brow. You have slowed down your walk, some of you are fanning your faces. Freeze.*

- *Now let's imagine that it's getting cooler. In fact, it's getting much, much cooler. It is actually very cold. Show me how you walk when it is very cold. Good, I like the way you're holding your arms around you, or rubbing your hands together. I like the way you have brought your shoulders up.*

Continue to alternate between walking around hot and cold.

Song

Ask the children to sing the song 'It's Raining, It's Pouring'. You may want to sing the song more than once and encourage the children to mime the actions in the song with their hands and to use their faces to show emotion and character.

Winter Relay

This activity is not suitable for very young children. Depending on its size, divide the class into 2, 3 or 4 teams. Choose a leader for each team and stand the rest of the team behind the leader. Ensure that the teams are together at one end of the space.

Place a hat, scarf, jacket and gloves on a chair or mat at the other end of the space. (Have only two objects for younger children.) When the children are settled, use the following instructions:

- *In winter, we need to put lots more clothes on.*
- *We are going to play a game where we have to put on more winter clothing.*
- *On my command, the first member of your team must move quickly to the chair and put on all the clothing.*

They must then run back to the team, remove clothing and pass it to the next person in the line.

That person must now put on the clothing, run to the chair, take off the clothing, place it on the chair, run back to their team and tag the next person in the line.

Continue until all the children have had a turn. The first team sitting down wins. (You can modify the game by having only one team who try to 'beat the clock'.)

Discuss

Ask the children to sit in a circle. When they are settled, discuss what they know about seasons, eventually focusing on what they know about winter. Questions you may like to ask the students could include:

- *Have you heard of the word 'seasons'?*
- *What does it mean?*
- *Can you name them?*
- *What season are we in now?*
- *What does winter remind you of?*
- *Sometimes it rains a lot in winter.*

FOCUS
Character Mime

Ask the children to sit in a circle and use the following instructions:

• *Have you ever played in the snow? We are going to play in the snow today. We have to get ready first. Do we need our swimming costumes and a towel? No! That's right, we need to dress in our warmest clothes.*

• *Show me how you put on:*
  o *warm trousers*
  o *a thick top*
  o *a jumper*
  o *a jacket*
  o *your boots*
  o *a scarf*

• *Don't forget a warm hat!*

• *How do we move when we are wearing so many clothes? Do we move slowly with extra clothes on?*

• *Okay, let's get on the bus.*

While on the bus you might sing songs such as 'The Wheels on the Bus', look at the scenery or have a nap. Make the bus journey as long or as short as you need.

Exploring the Snow

Arrive at the snow by bus. Once you are there, explore the many activities that are available. Ask the children for ideas. Expect a lot of noise, excitement and movement as they play and improvise. Bring their attention and focus back by calling 'freeze', rubbing cold hands together or using a breathing exercise (breathe in cold air and blow out hot breaths). Some activities may include:

• Toboggan rides. Set up the long fabric and get the children to take turns one or two at a time 'down the hill'.

• Build a snowman. This activity is mimed. Start by rolling a big ball for the body, then another ball for the head. Together mime lifting the head on top of the 'body', then decorating the body with branches for arms, stones for eyes and so forth. If children want to use an item from the classroom to make the snowman, gently remind them that we are 'pretending'.

- Go skiing. Again, set up the long fabric and ask the children to ski 'down the snow slopes' one at a time.

- Have a snowball fight. Insist there is no touching or fighting. You might want to try the snowball fight in slow motion to avoid collisions and focus on good technique.

After exploring the different activities in the snow, bring the children back to the 'bus'. When the children are settled, use the following instructions:

- *After a big day playing in the snow, it is nice to warm up with a big cup of hot chocolate.*

- *Let's all drink a nice warm drink.*

Mime having a warm drink.

- *Okay, everyone, let's go!*

As before, on the bus you might sing songs such as 'The Wheels on the Bus'. Make the bus journey as long or as short as you need.

- *We are home again.*

- *Let's take off all our wet, cold, snow clothes.*

- *Take off your hat, scarf, boots and all your winter clothes.*

- *Let's put on our pyjamas and our slippers and lie down and rest.*

FINISH

Play some relaxation music as you narrate some of
the activities the children did at the snow. Float the
long fabric over the children. You will need an
assistant to help, or select another child for this.
Then, as the children are resting, remove the fabric
and sprinkle some white or silver stars or sequins
around the children and tell them that while they
were resting it snowed. Let them wake and collect
the 'snowflakes'.

Extension

Winter is… Discuss as a class what winter reminds
them of. Divide the class into small groups and ask
them to present three images of winter. For
example: the children could say in chorus:

- 'Winter is runny noses. Ah-choo!'
- 'Winter is cold fingers. Brrrr!'
- 'Winter is huddling together.' (Mime huddling.)

Extracurricular Activities

- Make some ice cubes with plastic animals or
  other objects frozen inside. Watch them melt
  and ask the children to estimate how long it will
  take.
- Drink hot chocolates and eat 'snowballs' (the
  chocolate and marshmallow kind!).
- Make a winter picture with chalk or light-
  coloured pastels on dark paper.
- Make edible snowmen using white
  marshmallows with toothpick arms.
- Make snowflakes by folding paper doilies and
  cutting out shapes.
- Discuss winter around the world including the
  polar regions. Also talk about winter animals.
- Write about a winter adventure.
- Make a snow dome by gluing a plastic tree to the
  inside of a lid of a glass jar. Fill the jar almost to

the top with water. Add glitter and small pieces of white or silver paper in the water. Screw on the lid and shake. Sit the jar upside down and watch the paper and glitter slowly fall on to the tree.

Spring

Resources

- 'It's Raining, It's Pouring'.
- A long piece of fabric.
- 'I Can Sing a Rainbow'.
- A piece of soft classical music.

WARM-UP
Working with Fabric

Stretch out the long piece of fabric and ask the children to sit around the edges. When the children are in position, ask them to hold on to the fabric. When the children are settled, use the following instructions:

- *Today we are going to see what we can do with this piece of fabric. Are you ready? Hold on tight to the fabric.*
- *Can you make it go fast?*
- *Can we make it move slowly?*
- *Can we lift it up and make it move high?*
- *Can we lower it down and make it flat?*
- *Now let's hold on while we stand up.*
- *Can you hold on tight and make it go fast?*
- *Can we make it move slowly?*
- *Can we lift it up and make it move high?*
- *Can we lower it down and make it flat?*
- *Let's take some steps in and make it look small.*
- *Now step back and make it look big.*
- *Lift it up high again.*
- *And take it right down to the floor.*
- *Let's sit on top.*

Discuss

Ask the children to sit down on the fabric and, when they are settled, discuss what they know about seasons. Questions you may like to ask the children could include:

- *Have you heard of the word 'seasons'?*
- *What are the four seasons?*
- *What season are we in now?*
- *What sorts of things happen in spring?*

- *Spring comes after winter. Winter is a time when many of the plants and animals are resting. We stay indoors during winter and it is a good time to rest our bodies. But in spring, some magic starts to happen in all the gardens. Some people believe that there are magic fairies who visit all the gardens. Many things start to grow and come to life in spring.*

Spring Fairies

Ask the children to find their own space in the room. Remind the children there is no running or touching anyone else. When the children are settled, use the following instructions:

- *Now, let's make ourselves as small as we can.*
- *Can you slowly grow bigger, bigger and bigger? Stretch up on your tippy-toes.*
- *Now shrink down again, getting smaller and smaller. Again, let's make ourselves as small as we can.*
- *Can you slowly grow bigger, bigger and bigger? Stretch up again on your tippy-toes.*
- *Now shrink down again, getting smaller and smaller.*

Play the classical music.

- *Again let's grow up, up, up.*
- *This time can you start to grow some wings?*
- *Let's become the springtime fairies.*
- *Show me how you can use your arms and hands to look like wings.*
- *Can you make your movements slow and gentle?*
- *Listen to the music and find a way to move around the space as a spring fairy.*

SPRING

FOCUS
A Flower and Fairy Story

Divide the class into flowers and fairies. If you have a large group, include an audience. Place the flowers in a 'sleeping' position in the centre of the performance space. Arrange the fairies around the performance space in a 'sleeping' position. If you have one, ask the audience to sit in the audience position. Once the children are in position, narrate the following story:

- *Once upon a time, in a large garden, the grey winter clouds finally blew away and the sun was getting warmer in the sky. The magic spring fairies had been sleeping through most of the winter, but now it was time for them to wake up. The winter fairies had flown to another part of the world and the spring fairies began to wake. The fairies stretched their arms and legs, their backs, and finally let their wings stretch out. One at a time they flew through the garden waking up the beautiful flowers with their magic.*

Ask the fairies to go into the centre and tap the flowers awake. Tell the flowers to start growing when they are tapped awake.

- *When they had finished their work the fairies danced together around the flowers in a big fairy circle and enjoyed the perfume of the new spring flowers.*

- *Actors, please take a bow. Audience, can you give them a round of applause?*

Repeat the story and rotate the children to a different group, ensuring that they have a turn at each one. If you have an audience, remind them to sit quietly and respect the performers.

- *I saw many different coloured flowers in the garden. Do you know this song about colours?*

Song

Sing the song 'I Can Sing a Rainbow' with the children. You may choose to sing the song twice, encouraging the children to use their hands and arms to mime actions to the song. You may choose to end the class here or, if time permits, continue below. Alternatively, use the following part of this lesson as a follow-up another time.

Spring Farmer Story

Ask the children to sit in the audience position. When the children are settled, use the following instructions:

- *Do you know that it's not just flowers that grow after the winter months?*

- *Can you think of something else that might start to grow in the spring?*

- *Something that we eat.*

The children will come up with various answers; hopefully they will answer 'vegetables'.

Sit the children in the audience position. Select 2–5 children to be the farmers. Ask the farmers to sit to the right of the performance space. Select a further 2–5 children to be the vegetables. Ask the vegetables to sit along the front of the performance space. When everyone is settled, ask the performers to act out their roles as you narrate the following story:

- *Once upon a time, there was a farm. This farm was famous for growing healthy vegetables. One morning the farmers woke up and stretched. They put on their overalls and their big boots and went outside. They looked into the sky and noticed it looked different. They felt the earth and it felt ready. The winter had passed, spring had just arrived, and the farmers knew that today was the day for planting the vegetable seeds. They walked into the garden and began to dig up the soil. They worked all morning. Then they planted the tiny little seeds. The first farmer said, 'I am planting _____.'*

311

Allow the children, one at a time, to say what they are planting. For more experienced children, ask them to change their voice to become the farmer character.

- *When they had finished planting the seeds, they watered them gently. Then they went back to the farmhouse to have a cup of tea.*

The farmers return to their starting position.

- *When the farmers had gone, the seeds began to grow. They grew and they grew and they grew, until the plants had produced the most amazing, the most delicious, the most enormous vegetables. When the farmers had finished their cup of tea, they put on their boots again and went outside. They were very surprised.*

The farmers show surprised faces.

- *What did the farmers say?*

Invite the farmers to improvise a few lines here, 'Wow look at those plants', 'That's a gigantic pumpkin', and so forth.

- *Then the farmers picked the vegetables and put them in their wheelbarrow to take to the market. And that was the end of the story.*

- *Actors, stand tall and take a bow. Audience, give them a big round of applause.*

Rotate the groups around and repeat the story. Find new ways of narrating the story using the children's ideas. For more experienced children, ask them to develop a problem for the story. For example: the plants didn't grow, the corn grew too high or some rabbits came and ate the plants. Also encourage the children to find a solution to the problem and develop a conclusion to the story.

FINISH

Repeat the song 'I Can Sing a Rainbow'. Ask the children to identify something in the room of each of the colours. You may also like to group the children together who are wearing something of each of the colours.

Extension

Divide the class into small groups. Ask them to improvise a scene about a gigantic vegetable. Ask the children to find a 'moment of freeze' somewhere in this scene. This moment should come at the climax of the scene. Ask them to hold the freeze for at least three seconds. Show each group's work in front of an audience. Discuss the impact that the freeze had on the scene.

Extracurricular Activities

- Flower-pressing.
- Draw or paint a garden picture.
- Have a rainbow party. Ask the children to come dressed in their favourite colour or colours. Eat brightly coloured foods.
- Flower dyeing – sit a white flower in a glass of water coloured with food dye. Watch the flower slowly change colour.
- Bring a flower to class. Categorise its colour, shape and size. Discuss the parts of the flower, depending on the age group of the class.
- Plant flowers in pots or in a garden at your school.
- Mix colours with paints of primary colours. Explore the colour wheel.
- Make a flower using a pipe-cleaner as the stalk and adding layers of paper petals.
- Read and act out *The Enormous Turnip*.
- Bring in different vegetables to class and ask the children to identify them.
- Discuss how different vegetables grow in different parts of the world.

Summary

Resources

- Four large pieces of fabric or mats of different colours.
- Music for dancing.
- A picnic rug, or a large blanket.

WARM-UP
Energy

Ask the children to sit in a circle. When the children are settled, use the following instructions:

- *Let's begin by rubbing our hands together. Can you rub them even faster? Good. Now stop. Can you feel that tingling feeling in your hands?*

- *Let's rub them together again. Faster! Good. Now stop. Feel those tingles again.*

- *Hold your hands so they are almost touching. Can you feel that? Our hands can make energy. The sun also makes energy.*

- *Now let's imagine that our hands are the sun. Can you make them into the shape of the sun? Let's make our sun rest down low. Now let your sun rise right up to the sky. Hold it up and now let it set down low again.*

Ask the children to stand and find a place of their own.

- *Now let's imagine that our whole body is the sun. Can you get down low and reach to one side?*

- *And slowly let your sun rise up and hang high in the sky.*

- *And now slowly let your sun set down on the other side.*

This is a good stretching exercise. Have children bend low to the left, stretch arms up high and stand on tiptoes, then bend low to the right. Repeat two or three times.

- *And now let's imagine that the sun is very hot, shining down on us. Imagine that it is getting hotter and hotter.*

- *How do you move on a very hot day? Freeze. Show me your 'hot' statue.*

Musical Mats

Place four coloured pieces of fabric, or mats, around the space to represent the seasons. Identify with the children a particular season for each one. Play some music and let the children dance in the centre of the space. When the music stops, call out a season. Ask the children to move quickly to the corresponding fabric. Repeat with all the seasons until the children are familiar with them. Remove the coloured fabric and sit the children down.

Discuss

Ask the children to sit in a circle. Questions you may like to ask the children include:

- *Have you heard the word 'seasons'?*
- *Can you remember the names of the four seasons?*
- *What is the hottest season?*
- *In what season do we spend most time outdoors?*
- *What season is it now?*

FOCUS
A Summer Picnic

Ask the children to find their own space in the room. When the children are settled, use the following instructions:

- *Sometimes in the summertime, we go on picnics.*

- *We are going to go on a picnic today.*

- *What do we need to take on our picnic?*

Mime putting things into a picnic basket, using the children's ideas and suggestions as you pack the basket. When the basket is packed, lead the children around the space.

- *Can you see a good spot for a picnic?*

Let the children choose the best spot for the picnic. This will most likely be the centre of the space. Ask the children to help you spread out the picnic rug (or large blanket). Get all the children to sit on the rug and mime getting the food out of the basket. Expect a lot of conversation and improvisation. Encourage good miming skills as the children eat their food.

- *It is such a hot day today, even here under the shade. I can't even finish the rest of my sandwich.*

- *Shall we take off our shoes and socks and go down to the river? We can cool off there for a while.*

- *We will come back later and finish our lunch.*

Mime taking off your shoes and socks. Stand and walk around the rug.

- *Freeze!*

- *Now let's imagine we have become tiny little ants. Hungry little ants. Ants who can smell some food. There must be a picnic nearby. Let's go marching ants around this big rug.*

Lead the children in a march around the rug. You may also encourage the children to use their hands as antennae as they walk.

- *Ants, stop marching.*

- *Stretch out your antennae. Can you smell some food?*

- *Which way do we need to march now?*

The children will point towards the centre of the room where the rug is.

- *Ants, it's time to sneak. Let's tiptoe very carefully on to the rug. Can you see any food that's left over? It's a giant sandwich! Let's pick up the food and take it back to our nest.*

Allow the children time to tiptoe onto the rug, take some food and carry it home.

- *Freeze.*

- *Now let's become the children coming back from the river. Time to come back and finish our lunch. But wait! Where's our lunch? Can you show me your surprised face?*

Picnic Performance

Ask the children to sit in the audience position. Select some children to be the ants and sit them to the right of the performance space. Select some other children to be the picnickers and give them the picnic rug to the left of the performance space. When the children are settled, narrate a story about some picnickers going out for a picnic and the ants coming to take their food when they are absent or distracted. Your story might be something like the following:

- *Once upon a time, on a hot summer's day, there were a group of picnickers who decided to go out for a picnic. They spread out their rug under the shade of a big tree. They took out their food and started to eat. But it was such a hot day they couldn't finish their food. They went down to the river to cool off. Whilst they were gone, a line of ants came down to the picnic rug. They saw the food and snuck on to the rug. The ants made a long line, starting at the rug and ending at their nest. They passed the food along the line until there was no food left. Then the ants marched back to their nest. Meanwhile, the picnickers returned and they were hungry. But when they got back to their rug, the food was gone!*

Repeat the story rotating the groups so everyone gets a turn playing each character and being the audience.

FINISH

Repeat the 'musical mats' game using the seasons. Ask the children to move as either sneaky ants or summer picnickers as they dance in the centre. Continue to call out different ways of moving using the seasons as the stimulus. For example: ask them to move like it's a cold winter's morning, to move like the autumn wind or to move like a spring chicken.

Extension

Summer tableaux: ask the children to get into small groups. Ask them to make themselves into a frozen picture of 'A Day at the Beach' as you slowly count to ten. Now give them ten counts to get into a frozen picture of 'The Family Picnic'. Now give them ten counts to move into a frozen image of 'At the Ice-cream Parlour'. Explain that in drama, these images are called tableaux.

Divide the class into small groups and ask them to create a short piece called 'In the summer we like to _____'. Ask them to speak together in chorus then move to a tableau. They must present at least three tableaux in their scene.

Extracurricular Activities

• Draw or paint a summer picture.

• Write a class story about a summer holiday.

• Make paper fans by folding a square of paper in a concertina fold.

• Discuss the importance of water-saving. Brainstorm new ideas.

• Try tasting different summer fruits. Discuss differences in size, colour, shape and taste.

• Discuss seasons and weather patterns around the world.

• Create a sunflower picture by painting a circle, then ask the children to dip their hands in yellow paint and press them repeatedly around the circle. Paint a stem and leaf when dry.

- Create an ant farm and research ants and their behaviours.
- Watch an online video of leaf ants from the Amazon.
- Visit a local park for a 'summertime party'.
- Have a picnic lunch outside with the children.
- Discuss daylight saving and invite the children and their families to have an evening picnic at your school.

TEMPLATE FOR CREATING A LESSON PLAN

Title

The title of your lesson should be simple and reflect its content and purpose.

Resources

List all the things that you will use to teach the lesson. Consider music, books, costumes and props. Add to this after you teach the lesson, incorporating any changes that you may have made, to ensure you have everything you need for the next time you teach it.

Warm-up

Link your warm-up activities to the particular skill that you will focus on in the lesson. For example: you might focus on facial expressions, mime, using a loud and clear voice, working with others or presenting to an audience. Because each drama lesson is unique, the amount and type of warm-up activities will vary from lesson to lesson. Where possible you should try to include one physical warm-up, one vocal warm-up and one character warm-up.

Discussion

Discussion is one way of introducing your topic or idea to the students as well as engaging with their prior knowledge and understanding. List the questions you will ask the children to measure their understanding of the content. For example: 'What do you know about _____?', 'Can you tell me something about _____', 'What information do we know already about _____?' You may also like to show the children some images, pictures, props or other materials to engage their interest and stimulate their curiosity.

Focus

This is the main body of the lesson. It is where you explore the topic through drama, using movement, character, mime, learning and repeating lines from a story or text, investigating thoughts and feeling of a character and many other drama techniques.

As each drama lesson is unique, the shape of the focus lesson will differ, just as the shape of the warm-up will differ across lessons. When creating the focus of the lesson, the three components to consider are whole-group activities, story and performance or presentation.

Whole-Group Activities

Whole-group activities provide students an opportunity to develop their acting and performance skills in a safe and non-threatening environment. This is a chance for the children to work on their own ideas and to observe their peers, without having to present to an audience. It is the exploratory section, where the children can practise the skills they will use in the next part.

When working as a whole group, use language such as: 'Can you all show me…' 'Let's all be a…' 'Can you all find a way to create a…' For example: ask the children to spread out and all become the forest/make the sound of the water/imagine they are becoming the king.

Story

There may not always be a story in your planning for drama, but look for opportunities to narrate, read, develop or direct a simple storyline as the children work to bring it to life.

Performance/Presentation

Option 1: Sit the children in the audience position. Select a few children, between 3 and 6 to enter the performance space and present to the rest of the class. The teacher can narrate the story while the selected children bring it to life.

Option 2: Divide the children into groups of characters and sit them on fabric around a central performance space – have a different coloured piece of fabric for each character group. The teacher narrates a story, or facilitates the presentation, as the whole class works to bring the story to life.

Finish

Your lesson may not always require an activity or game to finish. Some classes will feel finished at the end of a performance or presentation. However, you may want to use a finish activity to end the class on a 'high' level of energy or, alternatively, choose a relaxation-focused activity to bring a sense of calm and order to the classroom. You may also choose to revisit some of the activities from the warm-up.

Extension Ideas

Extension ideas allow you to explore how you will extend the activity for those children with more experience, or for children in a higher grade/age level. Look for ways to create small groups (between 3 and 6) and explore the topic or theme using improvisation. You will need to give the children a starting point for their scene to ensure they remain engaged, and the scene has a focus. For example: give them a title, a first line, explore the element of time (a moment of fast-forward or slow motion), give them a prop or image to work with, or a specific problem to explore.

Extracurricular Activities

Extracurricular ideas help to extend the topic into other areas in the curriculum. Look for ways to extend through art, craft, science, literacy, numeracy, visits, excursions, cooking, indoor and outdoor play.

A lesson-plan template can be downloaded at
www.nickhernbooks.co.uk/youngchildren

MY LESSON-PLAN TEMPLATE

1. Title

_____

_____

2. Resources

_____

_____

_____

_____

3. Warm-up

_____

_____

_____

_____

4. Discussion

_____

_____

_____

_____

5. Focus

_____

_____

_____

_____

6. Whole-Group Activities

_____

_____

_____

_____

8. Story

_____
_____
_____
_____
_____

9. Performance/Presentation

_____
_____
_____
_____
_____

10. Finish

_____
_____
_____
_____

11. Extension Ideas

_____
_____
_____
_____

12. Extracurricular Activities

_____
_____
_____
_____
_____

NOTES

NOTES

NOTES

NOTES

NOTES